UNBLOCKING YOUR ORGANIZATION

Unblocking your Organization

Mike Woodcock and Dave Francis

WITHDRAWN FROM STOCK

Gower

Published by
Gower Publishing Company Limited
Gower House
Croft Road
Aldershot
Hants GU11 3HR
England

Printed in Great Britain by
Billing & Sons Ltd, Worcester

British Library Cataloguing in Publication Data
Woodcock, Mike
  Unblocking your organization.
  1. Organizations. Management
  I. Title   II. Francis, Dave
  658.4

ISBN 0 566 02854 9

Contents

Preface

'If you dig very deeply into any
problem, you will get to "people".'
J. Watson Wilson

This book is written primarily for those who operate in the world
of action rather than in the realm of ideas. Our own experience is
primarily in commercial organizations, where we have applied
the book's approaches across a wide range of industries. However,
the techniques described here have also been used in such
diverse settings as social-work agencies, police departments, the
armed forces, local government, and even in a convent. We have
personally helped managers to apply them in places as far apart
as Sweden, the United States, Spain, India, China, New Zealand,
Finland, France, South Africa, Hong Kong, the United Kingdom,
East Germany, Bophuthatswana, West Germany, Tanzania, The
Ivory Coast, Benin, Holland, Mexico, Canada and many other
countries. Through our books they have been applied in many
other parts of the world. We can confidently affirm that these
approaches and techniques are relevant wherever organizations
exist and wherever people seek to improve their organization's
effectiveness.

Our aim has been to capture practical ideas in behavioural
science and present them clearly and usefully. Guided throughout
by our own values and principles, we have included only ideas
and techniques that we have seen work. *Unblocking Your
Organization* does not offer you elaborate theory and research
data. We believe that development comes primarily from personal
experience and, accordingly, ideas that are understood only at an

abstract level are unlikely to have any lasting effect. This is the third edition of a book originally published in the USA. The text has been considerably extended and much new material has been added. Where relevant we have included material from our other published work.

The purpose of this book is didactic: we identify organizational blockages and explore their dimensions. However, understanding alone is unlikely to generate change. Companion volumes are being published which provide 'activities' to facilitate organizational development. The activities are the tools to implement the ideas of this book in practice. Because of the positive response of training professionals and educators, we have tried to broaden the book to cater more fully to the needs of the professional 'change makers'. Recently one of us spent an hour in a bar in Hong Kong, drinking Fosters Lager whilst a Sony CD hi-fi system played an EMI record pressed in Swindon, England. The world, so far as business is concerned, is becoming a global supermarket. This places new strains on organizations which face unprecedented competition and which must battle with increasingly sophisticated opposition.

No longer is it possible to adopt a strategy of muddling through and to enjoy a benign environment. Year by year business has become tougher. Only those organizations which are world class can expect to thrive.

It is not enough to be efficient and effective in just one or two areas. Each element in the business system must be balanced and the whole designed as a harmonious but dynamic entity. The social, political and economic pressures of our time force managers to become much more analytical about the organizations which they manage.

It is people who hold the key to success in any organization, because only people can provide the creative element that drives the enterprise along. Successful organizations are vital and healthy, they are ready to cope with the challenges of the future. They continually need to find ways of increasing their strengths and eliminating their weaknesses. *Unblocking Your Organization* sets out to help you identify and channel more of the latent strengths in people in order to benefit both the individuals concerned and the organizations for which they work.

Anyone who has tried to make changes in an organization

knows that the process is frequently difficult and demanding. Experience has shown that there is no point in trying to do too much too soon.

It is therefore important that we break down large tasks into 'bite-sized chunks' and tackle the urgent and important issues first.

In this book you will be introduced to the blockage concept. This focuses attention on those factors which prevent the organization from achieving excellence. We believe that the best way to develop an organization is to identify weaknesses in the business system and address these 'blockages' with dedication, insight and vigour.

Unblocking Your Organization does not follow the conventional notion that the best route to development is building on strengths. Rather we see the organization as a chain with many links, and which is as strong as its weakest link.

This book is unusual in another sense: we encourage you to collect data and explore what it means to your own organization. As committed advocates of the action learning approach to management development we believe in learning by doing. So, to practise what we preach, now is the time to curtail the introduction and get on with the job!

A note on language

For simplicity's sake we have followed the convention of referring to managers as 'he'. Not only do we recognize that many managers are female, we positively welcome the greater role that women are now playing in the management of organizations.

Mike Woodcock
Dave Francis

Acknowledgements

The ideas and methods we describe in this book come from too many sources to acknowledge separately, even if we knew them all. What we do know is that we owe an enormous debt to the researchers, writers and various trainers who have mapped out this field before us.

To some writers and teachers we owe a very special debt. Barry Goodfield, Roger Harrison, Stan Herman, Bill Pfeiffer, Henry Mintzberg, Warren Bennis and John Jones have contributed something of great value. Originally part of the structure of the book was inspired by an idea from E.R. Danzig and E.C. Nevis.

Finally, a big thank you to our typist, Jackie Davies, whose willingness to understand our illegible and misspelled copy exceeded all the possible bounds of duty. Our editors do a fantastic job and take enormous care to ensure that the result is clear and correct. Their work has done much to improve the quality of the book.

Of course, we retain the responsibility for all errors and inadequacies and hope that you will write to us, in care of our publishers, with your experience of using this book. This will help us to further extend and improve the approach.

MW
DF

How to Use this Book

Unblocking Your Organization is not constructed like a conventional textbook. Rather it is a workbook which can be used for organizational diagnosis and development.

It will help if we provide here a map of the book which shows how each part builds on the preceding parts.

Part One sets the book in context and explains how organizational change occurs. Many myths are destroyed as we explore the nature of organizations and the need for continuous reassessment and development. Whilst change is sometimes evolutionary and, from time to time, revolutionary, it must be undertaken.

Part Two of the book is unusual, but we hope that you will find it useful and revealing. We have developed a questionnaire to help you clarify which areas of your organization are most in need of development. This is not a test: there are no 'right' answers. It is simply a way of helping you identify which kinds of organizational problems ought to be investigated, understood and solved. As you know, we call these people problems 'blockages'. A blockage prevents managers from harnessing the intelligence, energy and effort of the human resources in the organization. Research in all areas of business and with all sizes of firms has shown us that most people problems can be described using the categories we adopt. The blockages have the same effect on organizations as they do on pipes and drains: they cut down the proper flow between one part and another, thereby decreasing the efficiency of the system as a whole.

We believe that discovering and clearing the blockages in organizations is the most practical and effective way to enhance the contribution of people. The most important and difficult step is defining your blockages and determining what effect they have.

Blockages will not disappear simply because you want them to; rather, they must become known and understood – 'know thine enemy'. Once the enemy is known, it becomes much more vulnerable. It is the same with organizational blockages; get to know them well; they are part of you, and once they are accepted you will have a much better chance of dealing with them.

Completing the questionnaire in Part Two will give you a rating on each blockage that may be affecting your organization. You can then explore and work on the most serious and relevant issues in greater depth. Your assessment will become even more accurate if you ask other people in the organization to complete the same questionnaire, thereby enabling you to compare different perceptions of what needs to be done.

Part Three contains fourteen chapters, each of which discusses one blockage in greater detail. By choosing the chapters that seem most relevant to you, you can work on exploring the blockages that are causing you the most problems at the moment and on which you would be prepared to invest time, effort and money in removing.

It is also helpful to consider which of the blockages is most relevant to you as an individual. Take the case of one manager we know. Polished and efficient, he was appointed head of external communication and customer service in an international organization. Soon systems were installed and decisions were made with an efficiency that was held up as an example to others. But good people began to leave, and dullards took the influential jobs. The output of his department become tedious and superficial. Privately, people admitted that they were scared of the manager's outspoken and inexorable logic. He saw creativity as upsetting the beauty of the machine; people did not dare to be innovative outside of his very narrow limits. Hence, this manager, who was so strong on conventional management control, was unable to build a truly creative climate. For him, development meant working on the blockage 'low creativity'. For a different individual, however, exactly the opposite may have been the case.

Further guidance on personal development may be found in our book *The Unblocked Manager* (Gower, 1982).

Part Four gives examples of the 'unblocking your organization' ideas put into practice. We present several case studies which suggest how to apply the techniques and concepts described in this book to the real world. Finally, in Part Five, we provide details of relevant materials, suppliers and organizations.

The 'unblocking your organization' approach has been enriched by the addition of 'activities' which are published as a separate volume.* An activity is a structured process for exploring an important aspect of a people problem. Each activity is indexed against the blockages described in this book: applying the ideas involved requires a programme of organizational development using activities and processes designed to address areas of systemic weakness or blockages. The activities are designed to meet this need.

A team approach

We have found that these ideas, although relevant to individuals, gain immeasurably when used as the basis for a team approach. If you feel it is possible to involve your colleagues, the following plan may help you to get started.

First, consider our ideas and see whether you agree with them. If you do not feel comfortable and 'at home' with our views, then there is no point in proceeding. Examine how you are feeling while you read. You may find yourself agreeing with our suggestions and experiences, or there may be something that you would like to accept but do not wholly believe.

Therefore, your first step is to decide whether the book is broadly in agreement with your own views. When you have satisfied yourself that our direction is one in which you would like to travel, ask for the views of a few colleagues in your organization whose opinions you value. See whether the book excites and interests them, or, to use a current expression, 'turns them on'.

---

* *50 Activities for Unblocking Your Organization Volume 1,* by Dave Francis and Mike Woodcock, Gower, 1990.

Since the will to proceed can evaporate quickly, one way to progress is to form a steering group. As the group is more likely to be successful if it is as widely representative as possible, it should first investigate its own views about the ideas in the book. A useful step in accomplishing this is for the group to undertake a systematic diagnosis using the blockage questionnaire. Once the results have been analysed it is helpful for the group to produce a statement of the principles it would like to see employed in the management of people in the organization. Once this 'statement of values' has been prepared, it is best to work on some activities as soon as possible. The energy for change will come from practical efforts which help people see things differently.

A few tips to increase your chances of success

We have seen many individuals, organizations and groups try the ideas in this book. Sometimes genuine improvement has resulted, but on other occasions it has been like pouring sour cream into coffee. There are no hard and fast rules to success, but these tips, some of them discovered through bitter experience, can greatly improve your chances of useful results.

1. Consult widely and genuinely to collect ideas and views

This is important for three reasons:

1. People have useful contributions to make that will improve the quality of any work.
2. By being consulted, people will feel more committed to any project.
3. By using people's talents more widely, you are putting into practice the principles that underlie this book.

It is easy to look upon consultation as a chore or as a subtle way of selling an idea. Managers frequently become highly skilled at forcing their ideas on others. Such manipulation, however, will undermine the whole effort.

2.   Start with modest objectives

Many schemes fail because they are too expensive, and managers do not have the time, skills, or patience to see them through. It is better to begin with a topic that can be grasped and handled by the people concerned. This way, results can be seen relatively quickly, and the amount of effort required is not felt to be excessive. In addition, the management team builds experience in handling projects and becomes increasingly prepared and able to deal with more intractable problems.

3.   Encourage frequent and frank discussions about principles and practices

To achieve real benefits, all those involved need to reconsider fundamental views that may well have become an unexamined part of their way of life. Such views change only if they are openly explored at length and in a constructive atmosphere. Managers ought to become accustomed to discussing matters of principle with their colleagues. These may include commercial objectives, but debate should be more widely based. Such questions as democracy in the organization and the responsibility of an organization to the community need to be thoroughly considered.

4.   Decide what you want to achieve and how to measure success or the lack of it

This has probably been said a million times, but it is rarely done. Well-thought-out objectives help make any operation much clearer and more effective. Clarity and agreement about purpose and aim bring a much greater feeling of sanity and meaning. By determining objectives you will be able to review the value of your efforts and make better plans for the future.

5.   Plan to learn from experience

In any programme of change or development involving people, review should be a constant feature so that you can continually improve the future by learning from the past.

Sound review requires that:

- results are evaluated
- reviews involve those affected
- results are made available to those who can learn from them
- honesty is paramount.

Outsiders can often bring fresh and unbiased opinions, so do not be afraid to use them in the role of reviewer. Most people will gladly give an opinion.

Dr Murray Dalziel, a colleague who is an expert on managing change, says that 'most technical problems are relatively easy to solve; the really intractable problems are organizational and managerial'.

The word 'change' is interesting. It implies that the current situation is unsatisfactory. New behaviours have to be learned and old behaviours rendered obsolete. Often the impulse to change is believed to be so urgent that thorough planning, even if possible, is not carried out properly. Major change is usually turbulent, frequently chaotic and costly. Yet it brings energy, enhances learning and is an essential antidote to organizational ossification.

The will to succeed

One further piece of advice about how to use this book: whatever you try, do it with conviction! We have learned that great ideas often founder because they are pursued without heart. Here are our guidelines for unblocking your motivation:

- transform problems into urgent issues
- don't generate excessive fear
- question all the assumptions: go back to basics
- maintain control: don't give away power to those unfit to handle it
- keep checks and balances in the system
- treat difficulties as friends: they have something to teach you
- treat everyone as if they can provide creative ideas
- become skilled in managing process
- be willing to say 'I don't know'.

Part One

THE PRINCIPLES

Defining Organizational Problems

Managing organizations is a strange and uniquely difficult job. All sorts of difficulties and dilemmas may crop up and frequently no clear way out can be seen. Any experienced manager is able to talk for hours about the difficulties.

All organizations have problems of one sort or another. Sometimes these problems are so serious that the organization becomes unprofitable, but usually they are not disastrous, and just act as a ball and chain to inhibit progress.

Listing all the various types of organizational problems that can face managers would reveal an excessively gloomy picture; it is most likely, however, that you will not recognize all of them in your organization.

Typical organizational problems

Scratch the surface of any organization and you are likely to find several of the following problems.

The organization appears to be unclear about its direction, lacking vision and a framework for strategy

It is much easier to write books about defining aims and objectives than to deal with them in business. All of the uncertainties in the market and in the environment make the job of clarifying the aims of business subtle and complex, yet the job must be done and company aims frequently revised. Failure to do so can lead to a peculiar business malaise that takes root and, like a virile germ, pollutes the organization. The illness has one main symptom – people forget the real purpose of their work and perform in a fragmented, half-hearted or misguided way.

Management values are unclear or inconsistent

Unsuccessful managements fail to share a collective definition of what is important and to pursue shared values. This means that standards are not maintained and key success factors are ignored.

Managers and management groups often work from principles that have the effect of creating anger, boredom and apathy in their employees.

Leadership style fails to direct and nurture the organization

At the root of this problem is the concept of authority. In many countries, the ready acceptance of traditional authority is increasingly being questioned. Often, authority and power are hated and feared because of their frequent misuse. Managers who treat people as units of labour to be restricted and kept under tight discipline find that the people so managed respond in predictable ways: they tend to feel little personal identification with the business and to seek an outlet for their unused energies – perhaps in leisure or in militant attitudes and subversion at work.

The management group lacks the competence to run the organization

We frequently find companies in a high state of panic because a vital job has become vacant and no one is around to fill the slot. In desperation, managers have urgent meetings until someone is finally selected as the best of a bad lot. Once appointed, many managers are left untrained.

Although attitudes are changing, there is still a belief in many countries that management is best learned by experience. Even organizations that take training seriously are likely to ignore the most senior group, and put power into the hands of people incapable of using it properly.

The organization structure is inappropriate for the task

Even when an organization has a focused strategy this does not mean that it will function effectively. The allocation of authority and responsibility has to permit the strategic interest to be realized. All too often the organizational structure is misshaped or inadequate, thus creating a wealth of problems that cannot be solved by individual initiatives.

People often feel powerless against the organization and may react as if they were caught in a thunderstorm on a summer afternoon – they run for cover and hope that the disturbance will go away. A poorly designed organization stunts contribution.

People and systems are not co-ordinated or controlled

We all know the manager who acts as if he were trying to steer an ocean liner by dangling an oar into the sea; somehow the ship sails onward, but no one is really in command. The concept of 'control' is one of the most fascinating aspects of management. Inadequate control results in confusion, apathy and decadence; yet excessive control results in fascism, fear and rebellion. There is no absolute way to know what kind of control is appropriate in a given circumstance; much depends on the individual situation. At the centre of the problem is the mechanism for creating and channelling information. Nothing is more revealing about a company than discovering who makes the decisions. Often there are a lot of surprises!

The organization hires people who are unable to perform to required standards

People problems sometimes seem to begin with the wrong person in a job. Almost every organization has its share of misfits, cranks and half-wits. Joe is too dim, slow and rude, whereas Mary is excessively flighty and inaccurate. Managers feel stuck with people that they never would have hired had they known the final outcome.

There is little doubt that selecting inappropriate people is the fastest way to undermine an organization's effectiveness.

People are rewarded for irrelevant activities or the reward system is perceived to be unfair

We come to the embarrassing question of money. Psychological satisfactions are food for the spirit but not meat for the body; hence, we find that ceaseless haggling over rewards is the soap opera of many organizations. Yet the most tangible measure of a person's contribution and value is his remuneration.

Pavlov showed us that dogs will learn all manner of unusual behaviours if rewarded in certain ways, and observation shows us that people in organizations are affected far more than they realize by the reward system. The most widespread people malaises are caused by issues of payment, because in this way people are weighed, measured, assessed and categorized.

People fail to learn the skills and develop the necessary attitudes

Managers often protest that new people take too long to learn a job in the first place, and subsequently fail to keep their skills current. Employees often leave before they become useful; older technicians, craftsmen, professional workers and managers frequently work with concepts that are twenty years out of date. There are a host of inefficiencies and added costs, including wasted materials, lost opportunities, training instructors' time and, with senior people, outdated professional practices, that affect a company's competitive position.

People lack challenge and excitement so they stagnate rather than develop

This is largely a question of attitudes and stances – whether people are open to development or whether they are not. We come across organizations that seem to be staffed predominantly by passive people who avoid challenge and are content with low standards for themselves and for others. People who misuse time and energy are out of touch with their own feelings and are intolerant to the views of others. These stances lead to low satisfaction with working life and low personal achievement, and any organization that is characterized by such people is unlikely to be really successful.

Communication is inadequate

Failures in communication result in four undesirable outcomes. Firstly, people do not feel part of the organization's vision; secondly, the work of specialists is not integrated; thirdly, the climate is unhealthy and, fourthly, those who take decisions lack necessary information.

People fail to work together in effective teams

Organizations exist to do jobs that a single individual cannot handle alone. Often, however, people seem to pull in separate directions just as much as they try to pull together. Management meetings are a case in point. Although, on the surface, a civilized attitude prevails, underneath jungle fighting, one-upmanship, defensiveness, muddle-headed thinking and sheer maliciousness are often in control. Important matters are rarely debated or even confronted because they are too sensitive, complicated or intimidating. Group members may lack the mental skills to come to grips with difficult problems or, following Parkinson's Law, they may spend more time discussing the purchase of a new coffee machine than the biggest investment decision of the year.

The organization is characterized by a lack of energy and commitment

Getting people to work is one thing, but getting them to work for the direct interest of the organization is quite another. We know of an engineering factory where the craftsmen spend most of the day as solemn as deacons and twice as slow; but they spring to life at lunchtime to make parts for their cars, lawn mowers and children's toys. Half a mile away, a manager of a group of computer-systems analysts noticed that his men had stopped taking thirty-minute coffee breaks and seemed to be working assiduously on new programmes. At first he attributed this to his motivational talks, but he discovered, quite by accident, that the analysts were developing a computerized betting method that should provide them with extraordinary wins on the horses.

When a manager finds his people putting effort into the true needs of the business, he can feel proud of a great achievement.

Creativity, innovation and change are poorly managed

All companies must develop new ideas and products to live, and genuine creative work is as essential as the annual balance sheet. Managers often find that the suggestion box contains ideas that would send the supervisors straight to hospital if taken seriously; and senior management often bemoans the 'lack of initiative' of the junior staff. Somehow, other companies always seem to have the good ideas a bit faster and to capitalize on them more effectively.

Common blockages

As you have read through these last pages, you may have recognized various situations which you have suffered in the past or are wrestling with at this moment. All of the problems and difficulties we have described are 'organizational blockages' that decrease the efficiency of the system as a whole, and all of them can be grouped under the following headings:

Blockage 1   Unclear aims

Unclear or unrealistic vision of the future resulting in an absence of coherent overall objectives.

Blockage 2   Unclear values

There is no shared set of values which contribute to high standards and fairness.

Blockage 3   Inappropriate management philosophy

Authority is exercised inappropriately or leaders have inappropriate attitudes towards people.

Blockage 4   Lack of management development

The skills of the key decision makers and problem solvers are insufficiently developed.

Blockage 5   Confused organizational structure

The organizational structure is unsuitable for the strategic direction or tasks which need to be performed.

Blockage 6   Inadequate control

Control is exercised inappropriately or based on inadequate information.

Blockage 7   Inadequate recruitment and selection

People are hired who lack the basic skills, knowledge, experience or attitudes that are necessary.

Blockage 8   Unfair rewards

Performance is inadequately rewarded or the reward system is felt to be unfair.

Blockage 9   Poor training

The latent abilities of people are not being developed to meet the needs of the organization.

Blockage 10   Personal stagnation

People in the organization are reactive and negative rather than proactive and positive.

Blockage 11   Inadequate communication

The organizational vision is not understood, co-ordination is weak, climate is destructive and decision makers lack information.

Blockage 12   Poor teamwork

Teams are not developed to their full potential. Individuals seek their own gain, meetings are ineffectual and co-operation is weak.

Blockage 13   Low motivation

People do not want to invest their commitment and enthusiasm in pursuit of organizational goals.

Blockage 14   Low creativity

Ideas are either not generated or not implemented.

These are the fourteen potential blockages which can afflict any organization and which provide a very useful framework. They are all concerned with human behaviour: other blockages could be identified which are concerned with systems, technology, finance and so on.

A 'blockage' is an impediment to effectiveness which undermines the efficiency of the whole system. It is the 'weak link in the chain'. Organizational development requires that blockages are clearly identified, described and explored. It is only then that those who can take action are able to undertake a remedial programme to remove the identified blockages. This book will enable you to survey your organization, to collect data on these fourteen blockages and to explore what they mean. This is the most important step. The companion volume will assist you in carrying forward a remedial programme to complete the unblocking process.

Defining a healthy organization

To conclude this chapter, we will describe how a really healthy people system looks. Perhaps a badge saying 'I've unblocked our organization' should be issued to chief executives who can honestly say that the following is a description of their organization.

1. There is a realistic set of aims which inspire people throughout the organization.
2. Management shares a common set of values which help the organization to thrive.
3. Leadership is firm but humane.
4. Managers are well developed people with all the necessary competence.
5. The structure is right for the organization's strategy and it enables tasks to be performed satisfactorily.
6. Control is in the hands of the right people and it promotes, not hinders, efficiency.
7. New employees are capable of making an adequate contribution and they have the facilities to learn what is necessary to be 'on top' of their jobs.
8. The reward system encourages high performance and is felt to be fair and just.
9. Necessary skills, attitudes and knowledge are developed at every level.
10. People are proactive and 'alive' at work.
11. Communication is effective from top to bottom, from bottom to top and across the organization.
12. Teamwork is practised and people who need to work together find that the experience is constructive, enjoyable and open.
13. Employees want to devote their energies in pursuit of organizational objectives.
14. Sufficient new ideas of the right quality are generated and implemented.

The Developing Organization

Organizations often begin with an idea and a person with the strength and the vision to build a business. Some enterprises fail in the early days when there are numerous setbacks and difficulties, others take root and grow. Often the head of a young business, a person of energy and drive, selects his staff with considerable care, sometimes from his personal friends and family. Together they form a good team, working well as a close group, finding challenges and defeating problems.

Increasingly, today, a large company will establish a new venture from scratch in order to combine the challenge and excitement that come with innovation and yet have professional management and capital reserves from the parent company. The vigour of a young organization often encourages an exceptional commitment from people. We know a new company producing 20 per cent more of the same product than its middle-aged parent across the road because of the additional energy that a new organization can harness.

As a business grows larger, it becomes difficult for its originator to plan, coordinate and control operations, while still providing it with the vital energy which is necessary to keep developing. Time after time this is a period of profound confusion. In a family firm, it often coincides with the transfer of management to members of the second generation, who frequently lack the knowledge, personal relationships and drive of the founder.

The way through this 'profound confusion' is to employ professional management principles. It may take a few years for information and control systems to replace off-the-cuff decisions. New people are hired after objective selection, rather than from personal hunch. Jobs are measured and specified, instead of being determined by the persons who hold them. Marketing, finance, production planning and control, transportation, training, buying and other functions proliferate and become separate units. Management may then try to overcome fragmentation by some form of unified procedure like 'management by objectives'.

While each of these developments adds something of value to an organization, there is a scorpion's sting in the tail. After a while, it becomes a massive task just to keep all the elements going down the same road. The system becomes so unwieldy and ponderous that it reacts slowly and clumsily to new circumstances. This is compounded by another striking feature – employees increasingly forget the purpose of their jobs and may lose interest in working positively for the company. When this happens, the system becomes an almost impenetrable obstacle. It is a paradox that the very ideas and systems that helped bring the organization out of confusion can become a heavy, smothering web of red tape.

This can lead to a second period of upheaval, confusion and ineffectiveness. In a way, the organization is suffering from middle age, and it can either rejuvenate itself or grow old in its systems, rigidities and disillusions. At this stage it is necessary to find the energy and clarity of purpose that were so characteristic of the early years, without losing the positive value of modern management principles. This fundamental task becomes a permanent part of the organization's way of life.

Managers can be helped by understanding how organizations are formed, grow older, mature and often degenerate. There is, however, no reason why an organization must die. The strong forces that bring about decay can be countered by preventing blind tradition from becoming the master of circumstances.

Organizations all over the world have gone through this development process and the problems that affect an organization at one stage in its growth are fundamentally different from those at another stage. Therefore, no single solution can be applied in every case.

Organizational problems may be divided into two categories: strategic and operational.

It has been estimated by business school specialists who studied the PIMS data base that sustainable success comes largely from strategic positioning rather than operational efficiency. It is useful to explore the relationship between strategy and operations for a few moments.

The emerging discipline of strategic management teaches us there are six significant issues for commercial organizations. Should any of these issues be neglected the result will be a strategic problem.

1. Identification of where competitive advantage really lies.
2. Raising the cost of other organizations taking your markets by increasing barriers to entry.
3. Tracking changes in the nature and structure of the industry and identifying emerging threats.
4. Understanding the basic economic 'drivers' of the organization and its competitors.
5. Developing effective strategies for resisting competitive threats.
6. Defining the desired medium-term position and building layers of competitive advantage.

Even when these profound questions are answered the organization has to be able to implement new strategies, objectives, controls and policies. Yet, as any senior manager knows, implementation is an easy word to say but difficult to put into effect. Why? Because organizations are a complex tangle of systems, procedures, cultures, personalities and structures. Every part of the organization is interdependent with other parts. Blockages can prevent any organization from working effectively and being capable of implementing new strategic initiatives.

Different organizations develop distinct blockages. A friend of ours is a manager in the China Light and Power Company where he runs one of the most modern power stations in the world. His tasks include assembling teams to tackle obscure and intricate technical problems and taking investment decisions which would frighten the finance minister of a small country. Key problems in his kind of organization are very different from those faced by another friend who runs a music company in South Africa. Here social issues, management style and artistic creativity are the key problems. The company would fail if he failed to sustain a creative atmosphere.

These examples demonstrate that not all of the fourteen potential blockages which were identified in the previous chapter will be equally important to all organizations. However the *process* of identifying blockages and mobilizing the energy to 'unblock' is important to all organizations.

How change occurs

We would all like change to be planned, tidy and undemanding; but in organizational life, development is frequently confused, untidy and difficult. In this situation it is helpful to know that one is not alone, that everyone confronts dilemmas both individual and organizational. Development occurs when we learn how to work positively with this difficulty, confusion and untidiness.

Most managers work hard to do the best job they can, but their love of order means that they do not readily see many practical ways of improving the situation, either because they have tried everything they know, or because they feel that there are too many obstacles in the way. Frequently, though, the limitations are more in the people themselves than in the situation.

It is easy for management pundits to give advice, but unless something is experienced by an individual as a need or a requirement, it is unlikely that change will occur. For example, during World War II, housewives were told that they could contribute to the war effort by serving unpopular cuts of meat to their families. Only a small proportion of them took the advice because they were not personally committed to action. When a similar group of women participated in an open discussion, however, many more actually cooked the dishes in their own kitchens because the discussion aroused their personal commitment. A need for change must be felt by a person before there is much of a possibility that something will be done.

Development also requires having a mental picture of how things will look when they are better. We need to visualize the final objective in terms that make sense to us, so that plans can be made to move in one direction or another. Sometimes a long-range view is not possible, thus increasing the need for a broad perspective to guide our view of the immediate future. The following example may help to clarify the process.

Mr Giant, forty pounds overweight, is flabby in all the places where it is possible to be flabby. He has not exercised regularly for years, with the possible exception of developing his arm at the local pub. He avoids climbing stairs like a cat avoids water. One morning he wakes up, faces his mirror, and decides that he wants to be fit. He has made this decision often in the past, but his will usually cracks at the first pang of hunger or ache of an unused muscle. But this time he is serious. In order to accomplish his goal, he needs to visualize the improvements he wants to achieve. Experience tells us that the more clearly he is able to visualize the end product, the more likely it is that he will do the necessary work to get there. In his case, although he would really enjoy looking like an Adonis, he will settle for something less than perfection.

Having established his goal, he needs to assess his present situation realistically. His naked reflection in the mirror may seem squalid and distressing; however, only by assessing his present appearance can he get the necessary information on which to base a plan of action.

Perhaps the most important element to effect change is a wish to succeed. Pious hopes and good intentions are like a rainbow; they are beautiful to see but disappear with the first change in the weather. The will to succeed must also be tempered with realism. If, for example, it usually takes several months for a man of Mr Giant's mature years to become fit, he may be able to better the average time, but he must be realistic about the scale of the job and give it the time and effort that it needs.

As we look around the office, the local pub, or the production line, we see many people who talk about getting back in shape but cannot manage to keep fit and healthy. Ambitions are cheap; genuine commitment to change is expensive.

The following straightforward and practical activity will help you consider whether our ideas about change apply to your own experience.

Begin by writing down on a sheet of paper an action of yours that gave you some real benefit. Then think of what led up to your decision to act, and how matters progressed. Take five or ten minutes to write down these points, then ask if your list reveals the following factors:

- there was a genuine need to do something
- you were personally committed to change
- there was a mental picture or visualization of how things would be improved
- some aims were made clear
- the task was sufficiently small to be handled successfully
- you pursued your aim despite unexpected difficulties.

If these points apply to your experience, they are probably effective guidelines to promote future change.

Development always involves some risk and initiative; often it means going out on a limb. Therefore, it makes sense to reduce the risks by being as realistic as possible. However, management should not discourage risk taking and initiative; although doing so may promote calm, it also saps strength and energy and tends to develop obsolescent men and women who delegate responsibility to their superiors as a matter of principle. When difficulty, challenge, risk and success do not exist, degeneration and sterility take root and thrive.

Improving your chances of success

One fine day in the country, a man stopped to pass the time with a farmer who was reflectively surveying his fields. Our friend said: 'There seem to be more rabbits about these days'. The farmer's reply was: 'Ah yes, there are more rabbits because there is less disease and we have had good weather for the grass. Last year there was a lot of fox hunting and so there were fewer predators. But they've stopped hunting the foxes this year because some of the hounds died, there are more weasels this year, and we've started shooting rabbits to eat, so next year there won't be so many rabbits'.

Our friend took a deep breath and said: 'Say that again, slowly'. To clarify the farmer's comment, he drew a diagram to show the forces working both for and against change – respectively, driving forces and resisting forces (see Figure 1).

Because the forces working to decrease the rabbit population next year are stronger than the forces working to increase it, the number of rabbits will decline.

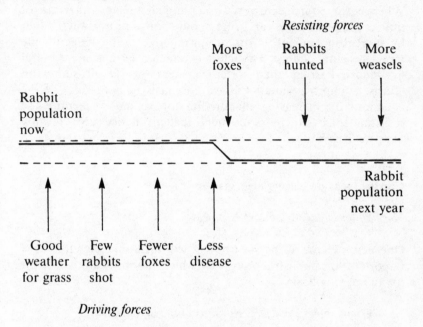

Figure 1   Forces for and against change

Similarly, in business there are forces working for change and forces working against change. The present situation is the result of the balance between these forces (see Figure 2).

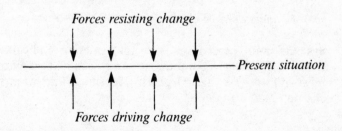

Figure 2   Present situation balance

When we can see more clearly what these various forces mean in practice, there is a better chance of bringing about change in the direction we seek.

Once the forces on both sides are named, they can be weighted. Whereas some forces are very strong and significant, others are of little consequence. We can bring about change in two ways; either by increasing the forces prompting change or by reducing the forces resisting change. Though it is often easier and more useful to remove barriers than to crush them, nearly all successful efforts to improve situations give emphasis to both sides of the equation. By increasing the driving forces and weakening the resisting forces, there is a much better chance of achieving constructive change.

Current ideas on change management

1.   Major change is an untidy process

One never knows at the start how it will turn out. Therefore, it is important to establish a *process* by which the top team can learn on an ongoing basis.

2.   Vision comes from different parts of the organization

At a particular point in time, the sales person who loses an order may have the most significant piece of strategic information in the company. Visioning requires both strategic intelligence and intense creativity. Organizations need a process for encouraging vision.

3.   Changes must be championed

Systems and procedures do not generate radical initiatives. Individuals with commitment and belief ('maniacs with a mission') are essential. Organizations must find ways to support champions.

4. Management must put the organization into tension

Change takes place when people feel that the old practices are redundant and can be improved. Leaders need to create tension to increase dissatisfaction with the existing order.

5. Beware: change is costly

All change requires investment. Structural changes are especially expensive. Managers are well advised to avoid doctrinaire initiatives based on fashion or superficial analysis.

6. The location of power is important

Power has to be devolved where strategies need to be determined at a local level to address particular markets. On the other hand, a uniform market is usually best addressed by a centralized structure.

7. Changes in one area affect other areas

As organizations are systems it follows that change in one part will affect other parts. The knock-on consequences are often not well considered.

8. Ambiguity must be managed

Too rapid change causes the flight/fight response in individuals. In effect, people become overloaded and become impediments to change.

9. Avoid 'death by 1000 cuts'

Change often requires reducing costs and pruning activities. Piecemeal organizational surgery reaps a harvest of low morale and destroys the credibility of management.

10. Indoctrinate and train those involved

It is important to win the hearts and minds of those involved in change. Persuasive communication is essential, but it should be reinforced by training. New skills give confidence and empower individuals.

11.   Management must retain trust

When organizations are thrown into turbulence the need for leadership is strong. People should be able to look at their bosses and feel that their future is in good hands.

12.   Opinion leaders need to be identified and led towards a deep consensus about ends and means

Research has suggested that about one person in twenty shapes opinions. These people should be identified and won over.

13.   'Positive' change must be rewarded

Change inevitably means that old reward systems need to be changed as these reinforce the past. A precise definition of new behaviours is essential, as is a system to reward success.

14.   Management must find ways to listen

No one can think of all the issues which need to be addressed in a complex change programme. Unexpected facts and feelings should be recognized and taken into account. A process for encouraging upwards communication should be explicitly established.

15.   Heroes have to be found and praised

Psychologists have demonstrated that change processes should be identified with individuals not with impersonal systems.

Seven suggestions that help change and development

We have found that the following suggestions make sense when planning change and development:

- visualise clearly what the change will look like when it has been accomplished
- take stock of the present situation so that you really understand what needs to be done
- make a realistic plan of action that will suit your needs and be manageable in your situation
- check progress and, if necessary, amend the plan in the light of your experience
- help everyone discover, in his own terms, what he should do as part of the process
- let people take risks as securely as possible and remember that sometimes innovations fail – new ventures need support, not obstruction
- think about the forces that are likely to resist change and those that are likely to prompt change – try to minimize the resisting forces and maximize the driving forces.

The truth of the old adage 'success breeds success' needs to be recognized. Where there is a history of successful change there is a predisposition to be positive. The opposite occurs where past changes are perceived to have been destructive. Negative attitudes slow down the change process, despite urgent admonitions of senior managers who seek to hasten the pace.

Wherever possible, it is wise to start a change with receptive users first. Once change has been successfully introduced it is amazing how the reluctant people mellow.

From one case study of managing change we learned the following lessons:

- the personal and managerial competences of a few top managers make all the difference
- it is essential that senior managers *really* understand the economics and costs of the organization
- there is only so much mileage in cutting costs – innovation is essential
- strategic review and redefinition acts as a template for change
- there is no single solution to big organizational issues – a 'mix' of actions is needed
- a close study of market segments is a prerequisite for strategy

- milestones (with measureable targets) are essential
- top managers need to change their own behaviour, introduce change programmes and make symbolic changes to communicate that there is a new spirit abroad
- objectives need to be clear, realistic, measureable, achievable and agreed by both sides
- whilst changing an organization avoid destroying too much history
- reward systems really influence behaviour – unless people are rewarded they will tend not to change
- a great deal of care needs to be taken to match strategy and structure
- the climate of the organization can energize or block innovation: it must be managed.
- individuals and teams must recognize that they have much to learn
- all those who are affected by the change need to be communicated with
- whenever possible, all those who could stop the change should participate
- people should be able to make 'an honourable mistake'.

Development styles

People approach change in different ways. Some, the 'dilettantes', involve themselves in random activites in a superficial way, never becoming truly motivated or involved. Others, the inhibited, refuse to take risks; they avoid all uncertainties, preferring to remain introspective and aloof rather than to face new challenges. Between these two extremes are the dreamers, involved in their imaginations only, preferring to create perfection in their heads rather than to build a better real world; and the discontented, always vainly seeking a magic formula that they hope will transform everything without personal effort.

None of these types achieves effective change:

the dilettantes – because they taste everything but never persist

the inhibited	– because they are never willing to explore anything unknown and different
the dreamers	– because their imagination and fine words satisfy their need for change while actually accomplishing little
the discontented	– because they are always hoping to find the magic formula that will bring perfection, and they do not realize that real effort on their part is necessary.

Our experience proves that although it is hard to avoid all the traps – and we fail to achieve our goals time and time again – it is invariably better to experiment and adventure than to stagnate. Life does not stand still. There is a saying that 'where there is no evolution, there is degeneration'.

Part Two

ASSESSING YOUR ORGANIZATION

The blockage questionnaire

Thus far we have described the kinds of problems that are likely to occur in any organization. Now we want to help you begin focusing on your people problems – the blockages that are important right now. To do this, we have developed a questionnaire that consists of 140 statements about your organization. Look at each of these statements and decide how true it is in the context of your organization. A rating scale applies to each statement and whilst it may be difficult to be absolutely accurate, it is most important to be honest with yourself. Answer each question even though you have to give a subjective opinion.

The more people in your organization who answer the questionnaire, the more accurate will be the results. Many organizations have undertaken a comprehensive structured survey using this instrument; and widely representative viewpoints are more likely to portray the actual situation.

Before you and members of your organization complete the questionnaire, you should decide whether to consider the questions in relation to the organization as a whole, a particular department, or a team or group. Doing so will allow you to make valid comparisons of the results.

When you have completed the questionnaire, we will explain how to interpret the results. By that time, you will have begun to identify your main people problems.

If you are an individual using the questionnaire, then it is often useful to review that part of the organization within which you have the most personal influence.

If you are conducting a survey with others, you should agree exactly on the areas to be covered. This may be a department, a section, a site, a division, or a whole organization, but it is essential that all participants share a common understanding. When you have made this decision, fill in the box at the top of the next page.

Prior to completing the blockage questionnaire

Write in the following box a full description of the part of the organization that you will survey. Consider all the statements in the questionnaire as relating exclusively to this part of the organization.

```
┌─────────────────────────────────────────────────────┐
│                                                     │
│                                                     │
│                                                     │
│                                                     │
│                                                     │
│                                                     │
│                                                     │
│                                                     │
│                                                     │
│                                                     │
│                                                     │
│                                                     │
└─────────────────────────────────────────────────────┘
```

Instructions for completing the blockage questionnaire

1. Use the Blockage Questionnaire Answer Sheet to respond to the statements. (If other people are also going to complete the questionnaire, it is best to photocopy the answer sheet.)
2. Work through the statements, in numerical order, marking an A on the appropriate square of the grid if you think a statement about your organization is true, and a B if you think it is partly true. If you think a statement is not true leave the square blank.
3. Do not spend a great deal of time considering each statement; a few seconds should be long enough.
4. Remember that the results will be worthwhile only if you are truthful.

Blockage questionnaire

1.   Inadequate time is spent on planning for the future.
2.   Senior managers abuse their power.
3.   The beliefs of many managers are outdated.
4.   There are no clear successors to most key people.
5.   Lines of responsibility are unclear.
6.   Standards of performance are not well defined.
7.   This organization does not attract the best people.
8.   People often leave for higher rewards.
9.   Managers do not take training seriously.
10.   People do not learn from their mistakes.
11.   There is no shared vision of the future.
12.   Each department or section acts like a separate empire.
13.   People show little interest in their jobs.
14.   Suggestions for improvement are not taken seriously.
15.   Corporate objectives are unclear.
16.   The organization's values deeply conflict with my own personal beliefs.
17.   Managers would like to revert to the days when hierarchy reigned supreme.
18.   The organization usually hires new senior managers from the outside.
19.   The organization's structure inhibits efficiency.
20.   Information needed to make decisions is not readily available.
21.   Too many newcomers are incapable of performing to an adequate standard.
22.   The payment system prevents work from being organized in the most effective way.
23.   Skills are just 'picked up' rather than learned systematically.
24.   Individuals do not regularly receive constructive criticism.
25.   Managers lack the skills of persuasion.
26.   Teams do not get together and solve common problems.
27.   Punishments are handed out frequently.
28.   Unconventional ideas hardly ever get a hearing.
29.   Employees are told to do one thing and judged on another.
30.   Decisions are taken without regard for the social or environmental consequences.

31. Management fails to create an atmosphere which ensures that most people are happy in their work.
32. Managers are not trained to meet the challenges of the future.
33. Parts of the organization pull in different directions.
34. Management information is not available when it is needed.
35. People with inappropriate competences are hired.
36. The organization does not adequately reward competent people.
37. Other similar organizations devote more resources to training their staff.
38. Individuals are set in their ways and do not wish to be disturbed.
39. Physical barriers (e.g. the layout of buildings) inhibit communication.
40. Meetings are generally unproductive.
41. People feel unfairly exploited by the organization.
42. This organization would benefit more if more risks were taken.
43. No one is clear about what needs to be done to make this organization excellent.
44. Top management often take decisions that are unjust.
45. No effort is devoted to making jobs interesting and meaningful.
46. Potential high achievers do not receive accelerated development.
47. Some departments are overstaffed – they have more people than their contribution justifies.
48. Managers are not in control of what is happening.
49. When recruiting, the organization finds it difficult to sort out the 'wheat from the chaff'.
50. The firm's total 'benefits package' compares unfavourably with similar organizations.
51. People are not encouraged to update their skills.
52. Many people opt out when the going gets tough.
53. Lack of trust in management is widespread.
54. Lessons learned in one department do not get transferred to others.

55. People would not be prepared to extend themselves fully for the organization.
56. Competing organizations seem to have brighter ideas.
57. At any level almost no one could accurately describe the aims of this organization.
58. This organization does not have a clear 'moral code'.
59. Management is not wholly committed to improving the quality of working life for all employees.
60. Senior people rarely attend courses in business schools.
61. All too often, important things either do not get done or get done twice.
62. Management control systems seriously stifle initiative.
63. Managers are not trained in the skills of effective recruitment and selection.
64. The organization 'pays peanuts and gets monkeys'.
65. It is not surprising that newcomers sometimes receive a poor impression of the organization, considering the way they are treated in the first few days.
66. There are insufficient challenges to the accepted order.
67. Decision making is flawed because views from below do not get through to the top.
68. Competition inside the organization has become destructive.
69. People are not enthusiastic about their jobs.
70. Once something becomes an established practice it is rarely challenged.
71. Priorities are unclear.
72. Management is not, in my opinion, 'fit to govern'.
73. There is a lack of leadership in this organization.
74. Managers are promoted without being given further training.
75. Some employees are overloaded while others have it easy.
76. When things go wrong managers do not know 'where to kick'.
77. There are few 'superior performers'.
78. The reward system inhibits constructive change.
79. People do not adapt to new circumstances quickly.
80. There is insufficient emphasis on 'self-development'.
81. There is too much unnecessary red tape.
82. People could help each other more, but they do not seem to care.

83. Many people are demotivated in the organization.
84. This is a dynamic age and the organization is not moving fast enough.
85. No one in this organization is clear about next year's aims and objectives.
86. The organization fails to make a positive contribution to the wider community.
87. Managers adopt an inflexible style in the management of people.
88. Managers believe that management development training has little to offer them.
89. Too many decisions are taken by people who do not really understand the situation.
90. Managers delegate without maintaining control.
91. Shortage of skills is preventing this organization from growing.
92. Issues about rewards are swept under the carpet.
93. Training is not regarded as a priority.
94. Strong individuals are resented.
95. People at all levels are insensitive to changes in the external environment.
96. Team leaders do not take steps to improve the way teams work together.
97. Almost everyone believes that there could be more challenge and meaning in their jobs.
98. People are afraid to 'rock the boat'.
99. We spend too much energy on unnecessary work.
100. There is a lack of clarity about the values this organization adopts towards the management of people.
101. Managers make pessimistic assumptions about the nature of people.
102. Management potential is not fully developed.
103. It is difficult to determine who is responsible for what.
104. People serve their own interests rather than those of the organization.
105. We do not sell the organization to potential new recruits.
106. The organization does not reward outstanding achievement.
107. People do not take personal responsibility for their own development.

108. People are not 'stretched' sufficiently.
109. There is a lack of personal communication skills.
110. Teamwork is undervalued.
111. Managers do not sustain a highly motivating climate.
112. Managers are not creative in their response to changes in the external environment.
113. There is no document which spells out the objectives of the organization.
114. The mission of this organization is not clear.
115. Short-term expediency is perceived as much more important than building for the future.
116. Top management does not operate as a team.
117. The way we are organized inhibits the achievement of results.
118. Managers are unable to cope with all the demands on their time.
119. Recruitment practices do not select the most qualified staff.
120. Many employees feel undervalued.
121. Top managers are insufficiently involved in establishing training policies.
122. Individuals do not take responsibility for managing their own careers.
123. Top managers are uninspiring.
124. Insufficient effort is devoted to building relationships between teams.
125. There is little 'fun' in the workplace.
126. There is insufficient creative capacity.
127. Planning is undertaken from an 'ivory tower'.
128. Organizational values are inconsistent.
129. The management style creates a hostile atmosphere.
130. Steps are not taken to develop managers as people with strong personal integrity.
131. The organization structure is no longer appropriate.
132. Projects are poorly monitored and controlled.
133. There is a serious 'skills deficit' in this organization.
134. People feel that exceptional efforts will not be rewarded.
135. Investment in training is not evaluated.
136. It is considered wrong to question conventional wisdom.
137. People feel that top management 'keep them in the dark'.

138. Team leaders pay insufficient attention to the needs of individual team members.
139. Success is not praised.
140. Change is feared.

Blockage questionnaire answer sheet

Follow the instructions given at the beginning of the questionnaire.

In the grid opposite there are 140 squares, each one numbered to correspond to a statement. Mark an 'A' in the square if you think a statement about your organization is true, and a 'B' if you think it is partly true. If you think a statement is not true, leave the square blank. Fill in the top line first, working from left to right; then fill in the second line, etc. Be careful not to miss a statement.

When you have considered all 140 statements, total the number of As and Bs in each vertical column and go on to the next page.

A	B	C	D	E	F	G	H	I	J	K	L	M	N
1	2	3	4	5	6	7	8	9	10	11	12	13	14
15	16	17	18	19	20	21	22	23	24	25	26	27	28
29	30	31	32	33	34	35	36	37	38	39	40	41	42
43	44	45	46	47	48	49	50	51	52	53	54	55	56
57	58	59	60	61	62	63	64	65	66	67	68	69	70
71	72	73	74	75	76	77	78	79	80	81	82	83	84
85	86	87	88	89	90	91	92	93	94	95	96	97	98
99	100	101	102	103	104	105	106	107	108	109	110	111	112
113	114	115	116	117	118	119	120	121	122	123	124	125	126
127	128	129	130	131	132	133	134	135	136	137	138	139	140

Total of As

Total of Bs

Interpreting the results

In Part One we described the following fourteen blockages to the effective use of people:

1. Unclear aims
2. Unclear values
3. Inappropriate management philosophy
4. Lack of management development
5. Confused organizational structure
6. Inadequate control
7. Inadequate recruitment and selection
8. Unfair rewards
9. Poor training
10. Personal stagnation
11. Inadequate communication
12. Poor teamwork
13. Low motivation
14. Low creativity.

In the Blockage Questionnaire you have been considering statements relating to these blockages. You can now arrive at your score for each blockage as it relates to your own organization.

The questionnaire has been designed only to give you an indication of where to start looking for the roots of your people problems. As such, it is not scientifically accurate, and the results could need further confirmation. However, from the experience of using the questionnaire over many years we know that it usually provides a useful guide on where to start.

Look again at the number of 'A's and 'B's in the vertical columns on the answer sheet. Score 3 points for each 'A' and 1 point for each 'B'. Write opposite the total points for each vertical column against the relevant blockage.

	Points	
A		Blockage 1 Unclear aims
B		Blockage 2 Unclear values
C		Blockage 3 Inappropriate management philosophy
D		Blockage 4 Lack of management development
E		Blockage 5 Confused organizational structure
F		Blockage 6 Inadequate control
G		Blockage 7 Inadequate recruitment and selection
H		Blockage 8 Unfair rewards
I		Blockage 9 Poor training
J		Blockage 10 Personal stagnation
K		Blockage 11 Inadequate communication
L		Blockage 12 Poor teamwork

M	Blockage 13 Low motivation
N	Blockage 14 Low creativity

The blockages with the highest scores are those that need to be explored further.

In Part Three of the book we take a closer look at each of the blockages and describe what they look like and how it feels to have them. As you read through the blockage chapters you should decide whether your perception of the state of affairs in your organization confirms or rejects the results of the questionnaire. Start with the two or three blockages for which you had the highest scores. As you read the descriptions of each blockage, ask yourself: 'Is this a real problem for us? And, if your answer is yes: 'Do we want to invest energy in solving the problem?'

At the end of each blockage chapter you will find a summary of the key concepts that will help you begin to explore that blockage and to work on clearing it.

Copies of the Blockage Questionnaire are available from:

University Associates International Limited
Challenge House
45/47 Victoria Street
Mansfield
Notts NG18 5SU
England.

Part Three

THE BLOCKAGES

Blockage 1 – Unclear aims

'A great deal of energy is spent on
work which is completely unnecessary.'
G.I. Gurdjieff

An organization that does not have a clear understanding of what it wants to achieve in a given time is like a ship without a rudder – at the mercy of the elements and likely to flounder in the first storm it meets.

Only by knowing what you want to achieve will you be able to decide on the action necessary to bring it about, yet time and again we see firms that have no clear idea of where they are going. Some struggle for years, complaining about economic conditions, resisting any kind of change, and wondering why their share of the market gets less and less. If they do expand, it is by accident or due to expediency.

The shop that is no longer located in the main shopping centre, the garage that remains on what was once a major highway but is now a minor secondary road, and the manufacturer who uses yesterday's materials and methods because he is intimidated by technological change are all examples of organizations that did not think ahead. Very few firms have a far-reaching, progressive plan that is understood and approved by all members of senior management, or managers who really have the opportunity to voice their opinions on where the firm should be heading.

It is not too difficult, with knowledge and experience, to establish a business that is reasonably successful, but the real test of sound business management comes when external factors change and affect the firm – when the shopping centre moves; when there is decreased demand for the product being manufactured, or when competition presents itself. The organization that looks ahead, foresees difficulties, seizes opportunities, and learns how to redefine its aims in the light of changing circumstances is the one that gets bigger and better.

The organization with clear aims will have a coherent concept of its identity. Each organization needs a 'vision' which articulates its nature and direction. Research has shown that the most significant leadership act is providing a 'compelling vision' for the organization. The vision acts as a foundation for decision making and channels corporate effort in pursuit of shared aims and goals.[1] Visions need to be expressed persuasively so that they attract employees who then make the organization's identity their own.

Top managers must develop a consensus about ends and means. This requires that functional responsibilities are subordinate to the interest of the whole organization. Once the most senior group in the organization knows exactly what kind of organization it seeks it becomes possible for them to be true directors.

A valid vision for an organization is never acquired cheaply. The following steps are essential:

- a comprehensive analysis of the characteristics of the industry in which you could operate
- an analysis of the structure of industry competition
- in-depth analysis of the characteristics of the most successful competitors
- an assessment of the organization's history and current capability
- a realistic assessment of the economic factors which will be an overriding influence
- a study of the organization's strengths and weaknesses so that real possibilities are understood.

Visions should be exciting as well as valid. Employees need to 'buy into' management's vision and feel a sense of challenge. Broad aims must be broken down into short-term objectives which present achievable challenges. An effective compelling vision has 'achievable stretch': it draws the best out of each employee.

Where does an organizational vision come from? The answer to this profound question is always personal. Someone, perhaps the founder of the organization or its current leader, must take a firm stand and say 'this is the kind of organization we shall be'. Equally important, the provider of vision is also saying what the organization is not. So, Ferrari is not a maker of popular cars and Woolworth is not a store for exclusive merchandise for the rich and famous. The quintessential source of a vision is a belief or a need. Save the Children Fund was established because a small group believed they could channel goodwill to the benefit of the world's disadvantaged children. In the early 1980s Alan Sugar, chairman of Amstrad, realized there would be a need for low-cost computers and devised an organization dedicated to filling this latent need.

A vision of the future is, to some extent, a leap of faith. Research, analysis, experience and careful strategic thought can reduce the leap of faith to a short hop, but uncertainty always persists. When IBM directors bet their company's future on the potential of the then unproven transistor they were making a bold but risky decision which proved successful and laid the groundwork for the global dominance of IBM in the computer industry. Think what would have happened if transistor technology had proved to be a blind alley. IBM would be an also-ran, probably a small niche player in a market dominated by another company.

The word which top managers frequently use to describe their vision of the future is 'mission'. The root of 'mission' is 'mittere', the Latin verb 'to send'. A missionary goes forth to preach the faith. A corporate mission is the identity of the organization which has been sent to inspire and guide people.

Powerful mission statements are based on deeper values than mere profitability and commercial advantage. As Peters and Waterman point out,[2] companies which are consistently high performers have leaders who pay explicit attention to values and want to feel a lasting sense of pride in what they create. Leaders know that their primary role is to breath life into the mission of the organization. Winston Churchill, President J.F. Kennedy and Martin Luther King showed us the attracting power of a mission based on values.

Mission statements can tend to be pious statements of intent.

For some reason many top managers adopt an attitude either of extreme brevity or reminiscent of a keen new religious convert when they sit down to write the organization's mission statement. Neither approach is helpful. Useful mission statements:

1. state the strategic driving force of the organization
2. say what the organization is not
3. are realistic and believable
4. arise from deeds and personal beliefs, not wishful hopes
5. avoid high-sounding and pious wording
6. are lucid and readily understandable
7. show benefit to customers, employees and owners
8. respect the distinguished history of the enterprise.

You will notice that mission statements should identify the driving force of the organization. This is a very helpful concept described in Dave Francis's book, *Unblocking Organizational Communication*,[3] where twelve distinct driving forces have been identified.

Each organization (or unit) should know exactly what its strategic driving force is, and what it is not. Organizations become confused and unfocused when they try to follow several strategic driving forces at once.

Twelve strategic driving forces

A strategic driving force describes the fundamental ways in which the organisation creates something of value. Each organization should direct its resources to becoming a good example of its type. Extensive research suggests almost all organizations fit into the twelve categories listed below.

1. State-of-the-art

This organization is devoted to being a leader in its chosen field. The state-of-the-art organization generates business by doing things in more advanced or clever ways than anyone else. The organization is a powerhouse of creativity and is constantly changing as new technology develops. Innovation is highly prized. Only the most modern will do. Customers are attracted by getting the best or newest goods or services.

The state-of-the-art organization invests in highly qualified people, advanced facilities, education, training, experimenting, and giving freedom to people (e.g. design laboratories, experimental treatment hospitals, research-based consultancies).

2. Professional service

This organization provides its customers with highly-skilled individual services. The professional service organization enables qualified individuals to carry out their specialized tasks. The principles and skills are guarded by professional bodies (like the British Medical Association or the American Bar Association). Customers are attracted to professional service organizations because they have complex human needs which should be met. Such organizations tend to be responsible and traditional, gradually evolving with scientific or social development.

The professional service organization invests in qualified people, providing them with support and resources to do their work. There is much emphasis on training and standards of behaviour (e.g. most hospitals, schools, social work agencies etc.)

3. Product producer

This organization is devoted to producing goods or services and offering them to defined markets. Product producer organizations have product ranges which are not tailormade for individual customers. Customers are attracted by products which are desirable and good value for money.

The product producer organization invests in market specification and research, product design, manufacturing, limited research and development, distribution and selling. It concentrates on developing within its chosen range of products and extending their attractiveness and market scope (e.g. mass production motor manufacturers, pharmaceutical companies, book publishers).

4. Experience provider

This organization provides people with experiences which they enjoy or value. The experience provider organization generates business by meeting a human need for sensation, stimulation or edification.

The experience provider organization aims to understand totally and fulfill a need or want. This may be for entertainment (a theatre), for excitement (an action holiday), for fantasy (a strip club), for interest (a museum), for spiritual experience (a church), or any human needs. Such organizations concentrate on the depth and breadth of the receiver's experience. The experience provider organization invests in careful market research, novelty, continued enhancement of facilities and a fashionable image (e.g. kissograms, Disneyland and other theme parks, St Paul's Cathedral and most other spiritual centres).

5. Market server

This organization fulfils all the needs of a defined market. There are many markets and market segments like fishermen, electrical contractors, stamp collectors or secretaries. Customers are attracted to the market server organization because it can meet most or all of their needs.

The market server organization invests in breadth of provision of goods and services. It is very conscious of its particular market segment and works hard to maintain a good relationship with its customers. It is alert to new needs and constantly tries to predict what its customers will require (e.g. electrical wholesalers, fishing shops, mother-to-be retailers).

6. System provider

This organization enables other organizations to communicate or coordinate. The system provider organization generates business by enabling complex operations to be performed. Such systems may be electronic, logistical or managerial; the essence is providing a capability to others which enables them to manage complexity.

The system provider organization invests in identifying needs for communication or coordination and developing both hardware and software to provide a wide range of systems. System reliability, cost effectiveness and system integrity are important. Such organizations are constantly extending the scope of their systems and their capabilities (e.g. electronic messaging, telephone companies, data processing companies).

7. Production contractor

This organization provides a facility for others to get things built, constructed, repaired, adapted or manufactured. The production contractor organization generates business by enabling specialist tasks to be done for those without the will or resources to do the work themselves. The essence of their business is that they contract to supply specific services which maintain or add value to products.

The production contractor organization invests in equipment, systems and facilities to do the kind of work that it specializes in. This may be workshop facilities, production systems, skilled human resources etc. (e.g. food packers, television studios, servicing garages).

8. Profit cow

This organization makes money for its owners. It is solely a resource for making profit and is exploited only so long as it is the best way of using the capital tied up in ownership. All managerial decisions are taken with the intention of maximizing profitability. The profit cow organization generates business by providing channels to exploit the commercial acumen of its owners.

The profit cow organization invests only in high-return prospects, and has no loyalty to any industry, activity, country or people (e.g. freelance entrepreneurs, asset stripping organizations).

9. Resource ownership

This organization acquires valuable resources and exploits them. There are two types of resource ownership enterprises. The first owns land, space, minerals, raw materials, crops, animals, or things cultivated and grown. This type generates business because it possesses and distributes commodities which others need and want. The second type of resource ownership is the large conglomerate which acquires a portfolio of companies that are measured on their performance. The portfolio is treated as an estate and adapted to maximize profitability over the medium and long term.

The resource ownership organization invests in expanding its portfolio of investments and harvesting what it owns. It seeks to extend its ownership to new resources. Research is done into the best ways of exploiting resources. Long-time horizons may be required (e.g. oil companies, large conglomerates, forestry owners).

10.   Distribution capability

This organization moves physical products to where they are needed. This may be by air, rail, sea, road, canal, space flight, mail etc. The distribution capability organization generates business by providing systems and vehicles for efficient transportation of tangible items without damaging them. It exploits its distribution capability in as many ways as possible.

The distribution capability organization invests in systems, facilities, comprehensive coverage, planning, specialized vehicles, coordination and communication, and start-to-finish service (e.g. international messenger services, frozen food distributors).

11   Maintenance of order

This organization maintains order. It protects property and services, people, peace and the rights of citizens. The maintenance of order organization generates business by enabling other activities to proceed unhindered. There are two types. The first is concerned with security. On the national scale the armed forces have this role, whereas local police, courts, security guards etc. perform similar functions at the community level. The second type provides services like cleaning, repairing, painting, maintaining, monitoring, inspecting and surveying.

The maintenance of order organization invests in predicting threats and having the capability to meet them. This includes the use of force, special expertise, trained manpower, dedicated equipment, fast response times and communication and control structures etc. (e.g. security firms, waste disposal, the police).

12. *Self-expression*

This organization provides facilities for members to do what they need or want to do. Satisfaction includes enjoyment, self-expression, enlightenment, comradeship, support, stimulation etc. The self-expression organization sustains itself because people wish to contribute and give voluntarily. Such organizations are frequently non-commercial.

The self-expression organization invests in its membership and facilities. Resources are allocated to create conditions in which people can 'do their own thing' (e.g. amateur theatre, associations of teachers of management, old people's day centres).

Identifying the single strategic driving force is a crucial step. Each form of driving force requires distinct capabilities. The organization's overall aims must be consistent with its underlying sense of identity. This provides necessary focus: a framework for decision making.

When it comes down to the performance of individuals or teams within an organization, the results of unclear aims are easy to see. One of the main reasons for low personal achievement is that individuals have no clear idea of the kind of performance that is required.

When a manager and his subordinates do not share a clear understanding of what is expected, the results can often turn sour. The manager makes false assumptions about his subordinate's ability and judges him by measures different from those applied to himself. The subordinate's efforts are misplaced. He is judged unfairly and, naturally, becomes frustrated and dissatisfied. In the worst cases, the subordinate can work hard but all the time be heading in the wrong direction. In the end no one benefits. It is not unreasonable for everyone in a position of responsibility to know what is expected and to have the opportunity of discussing these expectations. In the same way, of course, it is important for the boss to understand the feelings and aspirations of subordinates.

One of the chief inhibitors to achieving this mutual understanding is the gap between organizational and personal objectives. The organization may think it employs a manager simply to manage his department effectively, but the manager may have his own ideas about what he wants to achieve. In all probability, he wants to be recognized and to have the kind of job that leaves him enough time and energy to enjoy his non-working life to the full. No one pretends that organizational and personal objectives are in complete accord but, in truth, the closer they are, the happier and more effective the manager.

Another difficulty is our habit of seeing performance in input rather than in output terms. In other words, we tend to measure a man by the way he acts rather than by what he achieves. Rightly or wrongly, people are judged by how they dress, whether they make quick decisions, whether they are late for work, or even whether their desk is tidy, rather than by the results they turn in. Even in job descriptions we find phrases like 'he administrates', 'he organizes', 'he reports', 'he coordinates'. Until these descriptions are written in output rather than in input terms, they will inhibit rather than develop management performance. As one renowned manager remarked: 'Job descriptions are strait jackets and any manager who is worth his salt will write his own job description anyway'.

Researchers, having recognized the importance of clear aims, have developed a number of theories and training packages to help with the problem. Perhaps the most commonly known is 'management by objectives'.

The basis of most of these approaches is that a manager and his subordinate agree on what is reasonable to expect, how long it should take to achieve, and what measures will be used to assess performance. It is also important, of course, to assess performance and to use the experiences of the past to make better decisions about the future.

Experience shows that these approaches bring the greatest benefit when people work on their own initiative, without close supervision or support from above, e.g. the field-based salesman, the branch manager, or the holder of a key, influential job.

The ground rule is – the more important the job, the greater the need for clear aims.

A word of caution about planning

Plans and discipline can be invaluable, but often good intentions simply do not bring material results. We have looked at some of the reasons why planning tends to be ineffective, and we were not surprised to find that there are certain obstacles that strangle effort and effective planning.

Management indifference

This occurs when managers fail to support and participate in the planning process, often when planning is forced on them. Ultimately, unless a plan clearly affects the decision-making process, it is seen as irrelevant and it withers away.

Unrealistic expectations

These develop when managers somehow expect the plan to take effect overnight and to revolutionize the company. Planning is a continuous process, and it takes time to learn how to handle it with maturity and depth.

Defensive conservatism

This occurs when management is unprepared to reorganize resources on the basis of the plan. There should be an interaction between the plan and the systems within the organization.

Incompetent and irrelevant planning

Larger companies often employ professional planners, and smaller companies frequently subcontract a manager to undertake analysis and planning. When these people are weak, indecisive, or untrained, little of quality can emerge. A more subtle difficulty is unrealistic planning, often produced by eager and idealistic 'whiz kids'. Sometimes a work of business artistry is produced, but people feel that there is too great a gap between the vision of the plan and the reality of the situation.

Unclear plans

A clear vision of the 'castle in the clouds' must be supported by a realistic and precise description of the routes and pathways that lead to Utopia. Vague strategies, policies, or operating plans mean that the energy for change becomes dissipated in idealistic imagination, and little of consequence is achieved.

Ivory-tower planning

An excellent plan with well-defined objectives and action steps can still fail if the plan – produced by a small, insular group – overlooks the traditions and perceptions within the organization and thus fails to gain commitment.

Main concepts

- Clarity about aims is essential
- Aims must change as the environment changes
- Each organization needs to be guided by a 'compelling vision'
- Top teams must develop a deep consensus about ends and means
- Valid visions are based on thorough analysis of the organization and its environment
- Industry analysis, competitor analysis, identifying the main success factors, economic criteria and capability audit are essential steps
- Visions should excite employees, and stretch their capabilities
- Organization visions are an act of leadership and require decisiveness and imagination
- Visions are based on a belief or a need
- All visions incorporate risk
- Organizational visions should be expressed as mission statements
- An effective mission statement gives focus without being over-idealistic
- There are twelve distinct strategic driving forces, each requiring distinctive competences in the organization
- Clear aims are necessary at every level of the organization
- Effective managers establish aims, goals and targets which meet the personal needs of subordinates
- Whilst plans can be invaluable, the common obstacles of

management indifference, unrealistic expectations, defensive conservatism, incompetent and irrelevant planning, unclear plans and ivory-tower planning should be avoided.

References

1. See W. Bennis and B. Nanus, *Leaders,* Harper and Row, New York 1985.
2. T.J. Peters and R.H. Waterman, *In Search of Excellence,* Harper and Row, New York, 1982.
3. Dave Francis, *Unblocking Organizational Communication,* Gower, 1987.

Blockage 2 – Unclear values*

> 'A cynic is a man who knows the price
> of everything, and the value of nothing.'
> Oscar Wilde

A welcome announcement was made recently when Northern Ireland was chosen as the site for a large new factory. Why did the foreign investors choose a location which many would see as unattractive? The reason given was 'the work ethic of the people'. Despite all the problems and handicaps, factories in Northern Ireland are amongst the most productive in Europe. The beliefs and values of the workforce were seen to support commercial achievement.

Values are the key to organizational performance. Values also underlie many organizational problems. These days it is fashionable to talk about the need for a 'culture' change. Organizational culture is based on an informal value system which is expressed in behaviour. Culture can only be changed when values are redefined.

'Values' is a sociological term for 'whatever we consider important or unimportant, worthwhile or worthless'. They are shared in communities and are the foundation for objectives, standards, commitment and conflicts. What then are the values which lead to organizational effectiveness?

Our research and experience clearly points to one conclusion – that, in today's world, if commercial organizations are to be successful they must be able to:

---

* This chapter is based on Chapter 2 of the authors' *Clarifying Organizational Values* (Gower 1989).

1. *Manage management*   the issues related to the power and role of management, ensuring that the management role is clearly defined, and that leaders are able people.
2. *Manage the task*   the issues involved in getting the job done. Without sustained profits all commercial organizations will fail.
3. *Manage relationships*   the issues of getting the best out of people. Organizations are about people: the job does not get done without commitment.
4. *Manage the environment*   the issues of competing in the marketplace. Top managers must know the environment in which they operate, and seek to influence the environment to their advantage.

Managing management, managing the task, managing relationships and managing the environment are the four pillars of organizational success and, in order to strengthen the pillars there are main issues that must be explored and resolved. Clarification of organizational values is about resolving these issues.

We have identified twelve organizational values which are almost invariably present in successful competitive organizations. However, all organizations operate in environments which are, in some ways, unique. Additional issues may need to be addressed and other values formulated to suit a particular organization.

The twelve values form an integrated system. Their potential is fully realized when all are implemented with vigour and consistency.

Let us look at each of the 'pillars of organizational success' and consider the issues and associated values.

Managing management

Every large organization is complex, and specialist functions must be integrated for the organization to operate successfully. Only management can direct and coordinate this complexity. Success requires that the management resource is well defined, well selected, well trained and well motivated. This is what we call 'managing management'.

There are three principal issues.

Power

The management group has the knowledge, authority and position to decide the mission of enterprise, acquire resources and make decisions. Successful managements understand the inherent power of their position and take charge of the organization's destiny. They adopt the value: *managers must manage.*

Elitism

The management task is complex and important. The quality of people who fill management roles is crucial. An inadequate manager can wreak havoc – both sins of commission and sins of omission. Successful organizations understand the vital importance of recruiting the best possible candidates into management jobs, and continuously developing their competence. They adopt the value: *cream at the top.*

Reward

The performance of those who lead organizations is crucial. Managers need to perform consistently and energetically in pursuit of the organization's goals. Successful organizations identify and reward success. They adopt the value: *performance is king.*

Managing the task

Work can be dull, gruelling, demanding, challenging and worrying, but organizations are concerned with output, not the toughness of the task. The job must be done, and done well and this requires focusing on clear objectives, working efficiently, and not wasting resources. This is what we call 'managing the task'.

There are three principal issues.

Effectiveness

Focusing on the right issues must be a constant preoccupation. Unless effort is well directed, somewhere a smarter management team will find ways of taking your market. Successful organizations are able to focus resources on activities which get results. They adopt the value: *do the right thing.*

Efficiency

It has been said that good management is doing hundreds of little things well. All too often a small error makes an out-of-proportion effect on the quality of the whole. The drive to do everything well gives a sharp edge. Successful organizations relentlessly search for better ways to do things, and they constantly build pride in the job. They adopt the value: *do things right.*

Economy

It is a great deal easier to spend money than to make it. Lack of effective cost control is a common cause of business failure and organizational waste. The discipline of the profit and loss account gives commercial enterprises the ultimate measure of success. Every activity costs money; someone, somewhere has to pay. Successful organizations understand the importance of economic reality and that 'there is no such thing as a free lunch'. They adopt the value: *no free lunches.*

Managing relationships

Managers expect a lot from people who work in the organization. They want hard work, loyalty, skill, care and honesty. Such commitment will only be given to managements who are seen as being fit to govern. People should be treated with compassion, feel valued, and believe that rules and regulations are just. This is what we call 'managing relationships'.

There are three principal issues.

Fairness

One of the greatest compliments paid to a good teacher is that he or she is 'firm but fair'. Managements, by their actions, greatly affect people's lives, both in work and outside. What they do, and what they refuse to do, has great impact on the quality of life of their subordinates. The use of this power with compassion and fairness builds trust and commitment. Successful organizations realize that people's views, perceptions and feelings are important. They adopt the value: *who cares wins.*

Teamwork

A well organized and motivated group can achieve more than the sum of the individuals who comprise it. People enjoy the company of others and can work well collectively. One person's talents balance the weaknesses of another. It is vitally important for people to feel that they belong. Successful organizations ensure that they derive the benefits of effective teamwork. They adopt the value: *pulling together.*

Law and order

Every community develops a framework of laws which regulate conduct and provide the ground rules of acceptable behaviour. Organizations exercise considerable power over the lives of employees and their families, with managers operating as judge and jury, often without a right of appeal. Successful organizations devise and honourably administer an appropriate system of rules and regulations. They adopt the value: *justice must prevail.*

Managing the environment

All organizations exist within an environment – sometimes turbulent, often hostile and complex. Managements must really understand their environment from all viewpoints – social, technical, economic and competitive. Without this intelligence it is impossible to make wise decisions. In order to survive and succeed in their environment organizations must formulate a strategy of aggressive defence to protect their interests, take all necessary steps to be competitive, and seize opportunities whenever they occur. This is what we call 'managing the environment'.

There are three principal issues.

Defence

For many organizations it is a dog-eat-dog world. In every commercial organization talented people are planning how to increase their business at the expense of the competition. Non-commercial organizations are often under threat from those who provide the funds. Successful organizations study external threats and formulate a strong defence. They adopt the value: *know thine enemy.*

Competitiveness

The capacity to be competitive is the only sure-fire recipe for survival. Usually, this truth is readily understood at the top level, but it is far harder for the message to be appreciated throughout the organization. Successful organizations take all necessary steps to be competitive. They know that in the world of commerce it is the best who survive, and the weakest who go to the wall. They adopt the value: *survival of the fittest.*

Opportunism

Despite the most brilliant planning it is inevitable that unexpected opportunities and threats will occur. Organizations cannot afford to ignore the unexpected. It is wiser to actively seek out new opportunities than to allow others, more fleet of foot, to grab the best chances. Often opportunties have to be seized quickly, even though this may involve risks. Successful organizations are run by committed opportunists. They adopt the value: *who dares wins.*

Summary

Pillar	Issues	Values
Managing management	power elitism reward	managers must manage cream at the top performance is king

Managing the task	effectiveness efficiency economy	doing the right thing doing things right no free lunches
Managing relationships	fairness teamwork law and order	who cares wins pulling together justice must prevail
Managing the environment	defence competitiveness opportunism	know thine enemy survival of the fittest who dares wins

Value clarification

Clarifying organizational values has to be undertaken systematically. Much of the necessary information comes from the experience, beliefs and feelings of the senior management group. Value clarification is one of the few management topics in which inner beliefs are probably more important than external analysis.

Clarified values meet eight conditions.

1. *They must be chosen from alternatives.* Only values that have been positively chosen will be firmly held. The act of choosing strengthens commitment. Senior management must debate issues of principle in order to choose which values they are prepared to fight to protect. For such debates to be meaningful managers are well advised to adopt a comparative approach and study successful and unsuccessful competitors in order to discover the key values which are proven to lead to success in their own industry.

2. *They must be consistent with each other.* Values must support each other. Values pulling in different directions are destructive. For example, an organization that decides 'we will be technological leaders' cannot also decide 'we will not take risks'. This would be adopting inherently contradictory values. Managers have to study the 'package' of values that they live by, and check that they are intellectually and behaviourally consistent.

3. *They must be restricted in number.* Adopting an excessive

number of values dissipates effort and is confusing. Values should be broad, deep and general.

4. *They must be actionable.* A value that cannot be put into effect becomes a weakness: organizations should not be committed to impossibilities. Care should be taken not to incorporate pious hopes into values statements. This means that all organizational values should be submitted to the 'for instance' test. Cases should be tested against the espoused value to see whether it holds up in all situations. Only adopt the value when you are convinced that it can be upheld.

5. *They must be performance-enhancing.* Values are 'an enabling device', a means of shaping an organization to achieve its performance objectives. Value clarification is part of the development of corporate strategy. No statement of corporate strategy is complete unless it defines the wanted values – what is needed from people, and what is given in return. There must be a logical relationship between the main success factors and the values adopted. For example, an airline needs to be seen as safe and helpful by its potential customers if it is to compete successfully; so values such as 'doing things right' (efficiency) and 'who cares wins' (fairness) are crucial.

6. *They must be attractive and 'pride-giving'.* People should be uplifted by an organization's values. They should feel pride when playing a part in making a performance objective become reality. The values advocated by management must touch a deep chord within people at all levels. Values must be capable of being respected. People feel part of a greater whole when they can identify with the organization's goals.

7. *They must be capable of being communicated.* It is what managers do – symbolic communication – that is vital. Managers' actions must reinforce their value statements. An important management task is translating values into terms that are meaningful to each individual. Managers should not adopt a value unless it is capable of being demonstrated. This means that the first group to adopt a value must be managers themselves. From time to time managers are well advised to collect data from below to see what messages their behaviour is communicating.

8. *They must be written down.* Until a set of values is clear enough to be committed to paper it will not have the

authority to be a respected statement. The act of writing down values has three benefits: it clarifies minds; provokes debate and provides a message which can be communicated. It is the task of senior managers, those at the apex of the organization, to explore their own and their competitors' values and determine those that will provide the foundation for the organization's future. When they are written down any logical flaws will then appear!

Key concepts

- Values may be simply defined as 'what people consider important and worthwhile'
- Values are the foundation of behaviour, and are of vital importance to managers
- There are four pillars of organizational success – managing management, managing the task, managing relationships and managing the environment
- Twelve values can be identified which are almost invariably associated with consistently successful commercial organizations
- The first value is 'managers must manage' and is derived from a consideration of how power is exercised in organizations
- The second value is 'cream at the top' and is derived from a consideration of elitism in organizations
- The third value is 'performance is king' and is derived from a consideration of the reward system
- The fourth value is 'do the right thing' and is derived from a consideration of how effectiveness is achieved
- The fifth value is 'do things right' and is derived from the need to be efficient
- The sixth value is 'no free lunches' and is derived from a consideration of how to use resources economically
- The seventh value is 'who cares wins' and is derived from the need to be fair and compassionate
- The eighth value is 'pulling together' and is based on the advantages of teamwork

- The ninth value, 'justice must prevail', stems from the need to have a system of law and order
- The tenth value 'know thine enemy' is derived from a consideration of defence strategy
- The eleventh value 'survival of the fittest' stems from the need to be competitive
- The twelfth value 'who dares wins' is derived from a consideration of how to deal with the unexpected
- Values form an integrated system – their potential is fully realized when all are implemented with vigour and consistency
- Clarified values are

  - chosen from alternatives
  - consistent with each other
  - restricted in number
  - actionable
  - performance-enhancing
  - attractive and 'pride-giving'
  - capable of being communicated
  - written down.

Blockage 3 – Inappropriate management philosophy

> 'This above all; to thine own self be true,
> And it must follow, as the night the day,
> Thou canst not then be false to any man.'
> Shakespeare

In a resort town on the coast, there is a large old hotel that caters mainly for tourists and business conventions. One of the waiters, a foreigner who has not completely mastered the English language, tends to get confused at times, especially when the dining room is very busy. As a result, not only do customers often have to wait a long time for their food, but when it does arrive, it turns out to be fish instead of steak, accompanied by Worcestershire instead of tartare sauce. Watching how customers cope with that waiter is an education in itself. Some turn purple and bang and shout and generally insult him. A few others, who seem to understand his problem, try patiently to communicate, or call over another waiter who looks as if he could speak English. The rest, by far the majority, do not seem to know what to do, so they sit and eat their fish and Worcestershire sauce without comment or complaint.

Whenever people face challenges, they generally respond in one of three ways:

1. By fighting, like those who shouted at the waiter. Unfortunately, in this case, the waiter became more confused and the shouters probably got so incensed that anger spoiled their meal.
2. By avoiding or not facing the issue, like the people who accepted their fish and Worcestershire sauce. This type of response results in an apparently quiet, amiable existence,

but it does not solve any underlying problems which may accumulate and eventually overwhelm the passive avoider.

3. By trying to work constructively on the problem, like the few who patiently tried to communicate or called over an English-speaking waiter. These were the people who eventually solved their problem and were served the right food.

When a manager fights, the situation is often turned into a trial of strength, or into a win-lose situation. The losers creep away to lick their wounds and learn to avoid future confrontations. Managers who fight this way use fear to get things done. In the short term, results are often quite good, but they depend on the ability, ideas and capacity of one man. In the long run, though, others find their own ways of avoiding delicate areas by walking on safe ground. If no one is willing to take a risk, the potential contribution that employees can make is never harnessed and, as a result, the organization loses.

When a manager avoids an issue, and continues to sweep problems under the carpet, those problems get larger. Unlike the manager who fights, this one will not usually be feared, but neither will he be respected. And, because issues are not faced, people will not usually raise them.

When a manager tries to work constructively on issues, people are much more likely to raise their own problems and ideas with him, thus maximizing everyone's contribution. This way of working offers the best prospect of using the hidden potential of people.

Assumptions about human nature

Most effective organizations place a high premium on a management philosophy that encourages openness, probing, honesty, and a desire to face problems and to work constructively on solving them. This relates to our assumptions about the nature of people.

Because these matters are more a question of deep feeling than of superficial thought, some managers, not surprisingly, see them as more relevant to the psychiatrist's couch than to the boardroom. But many individual managers and organizations have found it extremely beneficial to consider their own fundamental beliefs in relation to their management philosophy.

To accomplish this, we begin with straightforward ideas developed by Douglas McGregor, who found that the behaviour a manager exhibited told a great deal about the way he or she valued other people and the assumptions made about them.

Managers in the first camp shared a view about people that McGregor called 'Theory X'. They believed that people:

- were fundamentally lazy and had to be pushed to work
- were basically sly and interested only in their own benefit
- responded best when disciplined and controlled
- took notice of punishment and worked harder because of it
- were essentially not interested in their jobs and worked against their will.

The other camp, 'Theory Y', took a diametrically opposed view. They believed that people:

- were fundamentally willing to work on meaningful tasks
- were basically honest and interested in the welfare of the group to which they belonged
- responded best when given responsibility and some freedom to make their own decisions
- took notice of honest praise and resented excessive punishment
- were essentially interested in the quality of their professional and personal lives.

McGregor pointed out that we act from our model of the world and so the basic values and beliefs which a manager holds become elaborated into his style. Of course, a style evokes a response. Theory X managers treat people as untrustworthy and the subordinates often then behave as expected. Theory Y managers produce a different response. People often behave honestly and willingly when led in this way. The style adopted by a manager tends to evoke the response he expects: the values adopted become a self-fulfilling prophecy.

McGregor's views have been developed by Paul Hersey and Ken Blanchard who emphasize that management style should be related to the 'readiness' of those being managed.

Their approach – known as 'situational leadership' – is valued as practical and relevant by many managers. According to Hersey and Blanchard,[2] an effective manager learns to diagnose the leadership needs of complex situations and skilfully apply the appropriate style. We have drawn from Hersey and Blanchard in describing the following four styles of management behaviour.

Telling

What it is: the leader instructs carefully and watches task performance, remaining very involved in the detail of what is going on. Inadequate performance and unsatisfactory standards are quickly identified and pointed out to the person held responsible. The leader makes it quite clear what is expected and insists on improvement, placing emphasis on individual skill development.

When to use it: the telling style of leadership is applied to individuals and groups who are unable to tackle the task and lack the will to learn for themselves. The approach is especially useful with new recruits or when taking over departments that have been allowed to 'go to seed'.

What to do:

- be clear about your standards
- instruct extensively
- develop individual's technical skills
- check performance
- discipline when necessary
- point out errors and good work
- develop pride in good performance
- be considerate but firm
- emphasize performance, and
- help learning by showing interest in learning problems.

Selling

What it is: the leader takes frequent initiatives and is very active in directing, instructing and monitoring performance. Communication is given a high priority and the leader invests energy in getting acquainted with individuals and in developing rapport with them. Much attention is given to performance standards and the employees are involved in setting them. The relevance of people's work is discussed, and their performance is related to the organization.

When to use it: the selling leadership style is used with more established groups and individuals who have certain basic skills but still have much to learn. The style is well-suited to groups whose members are willing but need to care more about their work. The selling approach is also useful with groups that have quality or production problems they are unable to solve. The leader's emphasis on control and instruction develops workers' skills in a systematic manner.

What to do:

- spend time with each individual
- identify topics of common interest
- assess individual character
- communicate extensively
- develop pride in output
- be directive whenever necessary
- monitor performance according to standards
- discipline to maintain standards and
- reward positive behaviour.

Participating

What it is: the leader focuses on improving the morale and spirit of the group and is active in developing personal relationships and encouraging participation. People are taught to tackle and solve their own problems. Direction is kept to a minimum, although exceptional circumstances are clarified and decided by the manager. Care is taken to see that important decisions are fully explained, and the leader encourages the group members to make a contribution to the wider organization.

When to use it: the participating leadership style is used with individuals and groups who have the basic skills and competence to handle most of the technical aspects of the job. Further development of such a group requires that the members take more responsibility for their day-to-day work and keep their own morale high.

What to do:

- limit direction and control
- set up self-monitoring systems
- counsel on problems
- develop people by coaching assignments
- communicate widely
- encourage comment and feedback
- communicate objectives without specifying how they will be achieved, and
- give increasing responsibility.

Delegating

What it is: the leader acts as a resource but leaves much of the work to the individual group members. Day-to-day monitoring and control is administered by the group members.

When to use it: the delegating leadership style is used with individuals or groups who have achieved a competent level of skills and are willing to devote their energies to doing a good job. The style is appropriate to managing competent people who have responsible and positive attitudes toward their organizations.

What to do:

- clarify and agree on objectives
- give support when requested
- represent the group to others if necessary
- avoid interfering
- respond to requests seriously.

Developmental stages

Individuals and groups go through a number of development stages, and the effective leader will identify what each needs at a particular time. This process is more complex than it appears. Some individuals lack either the willingness or the ability to learn a job or to handle it. The style of leadership appropriate for them is very different from that required by willing and able people.

The effective leader helps a group progress to a high level of responsibility and competence. In order to do this, the insightful manager will want to know: (a) where the group's development is at the moment; (b) how the group is likely to progress; and (c) what the leader can do to help.

Insightful leadership meets the needs of people; is appropriate to their personalities and to their level of job competence; and is also a genuine expression of a manager's personal beliefs. Trying to assume a style that is foreign to your personality is usually a mistake. However, it is possible to learn how to present different aspects of yourself and to discriminate when these are useful and appropriate. A delicate balance is required to avoid manipulation and a false stance of superiority, since such behaviours provoke group members to view the leader with resentment and lack of trust. Always consider the needs of the people being managed. Sometimes they need to be supported, sometimes directed, sometimes disciplined, and sometimes faced with unpleasant information about their positions. Their skills morale and sense of group identity are greatly affected by the way their manager chooses to behave toward them.

Leadership, like honour, is hard to identify with precision. Different approaches to leadership are adopted for reasons of personal preference, local custom, and the nature of the tasks being performed and the people performing them. One manager may display symbols of an elevated status – lush carpets, longer lunch breaks, and an immaculately groomed and underworked secretary. Another may exhibit an open style toward subordinates, welcoming direct expression and scorning status symbols that act as barriers between supervisors and subordinates. Differences and problems can become sources of strength if they are dealt with in an open and effective problem-solving way. It is a primary task of managers and supervisors to ensure that this process happens and that issues are raised, clarified and worked through to resolution.

Later work has emphasized the importance of 'vision'. Warren Bennis has conducted an extensive study of ninety very successful leaders.[3]

Bennis defines leadership as 'The capacity to create a compelling vision and translate it into action and sustain it'. Bennis spent time with ninety of America's leaders, including Neil Armstrong, the coach of the Los Angeles Rams, orchestral conductors, and businessmen such as Ray Kroc of McDonalds and William Kieschnick, chief executive of ARCO.

Links between such a diverse group of successful leaders were difficult to establish.

'They were right-brained and left-brained, tall and short, fat and thin, articulate and inarticulate, assertive and retiring, dressed for success and dressed for failure, participative and autocratic', he wrote.

Four common abilities were identified: management of attention; of meaning; of trust; and of self. Bennis points out that this bears out Tolstoy's famous opening lines in *Anna Karenina:* 'All happy families resemble each other while each unhappy family is unhappy in its own way.'

Social and human responsibility

Even though the social responsibility of organizations is a fashionable subject today, it is still genuinely significant. Especially relevant to managers is the effect of business decisions on human communities and on the natural world.

Some businesses and other organizations have used their resources to reduce pollution, serve the community, assist social problems and conflicts, give responsible service to consumers, aid stable economic patterns, provide healthy conditions for employees, structure work to aid psychological satisfaction, support those in difficulty, and prepare individuals for the challenges of the future.

Creation of wealth for its own sake is a highly questionable and shallow aim. The question must be asked, 'Wealth for whom, and for what purpose?' And, perhaps more basically, 'What is wealth?'

These are fundamental questions that must be asked by everyone with power and responsibility. The answers are far from easy, but the fact that they are debated leads to a deepening of management quality.

We conclude by making an analogy between management and politics. An organization is a community which needs good government. Someone has to look after relationships, law and order, defence, economics, education and so on. Politicians thrive only when they have an attractive and coherent philosophy which results in sustained success. Managers require the same political skills and must take a positive stance. Fence sitting and cowardice are strategies for the doldrums. Management values are a greatly under-considered topic.

Key concepts

- Fight and flight are both destructive reactions: managers must confront problems positively
- Assumptions about the nature of man affect management philosophy
- Douglas McGregor extended our thinking with his 'Theory X', 'Theory Y' approach
- Philosophies of management tend to be self-fulfilling prophecies
- The situational leadership approach of Hersey and Blanchard provides an insight into the importance of reacting appropriately to the situation
- There are four basic management styles: telling, selling, participating and delegating
- Leadership styles need to be authentic: wholly believed in by the manager
- Leadership is usefully defined as 'the capacity to create a compelling vision, translate it into action and sustain it'
- Organizational leadership is similar to politics. Senior managers cannot sit on the fence – they must develop a coherent philosophy.

References

1. D. McGregor, *The Human Side of the Enterprise*, McGraw-Hill, New York, 1960.
2. Hersey and Blanchard, *Organizational Change through Effective Leadership*, Prentice-Hall, Hemel Hempstead, 1977.
3. Bennis, W.G. and Nanus, B. *Leaders: the Strategies for Taking Charge*, Harper and Row, New York, 1985.

Blockage 4 - Lack of management development

Nobody plans to fail
but many fail to plan

Organizations which have been consistently successful over many years always give careful attention to two things: preparing for the future and developing each individual's capabilities.

Many organizations seem to stumble through their management development problems. Although too much planning can lead to problems, it is important to determine the degree that is relevant.

One firm we know suddenly came face to face with a big succession problem. It operated over 100 retail shops, most of which were managed by people in their fifties. When these managers first came into the business, retailing was seen as a good job, and young people were eager to enter the business. Only when these managers began to retire did the firm suddenly realize that it had a problem. For years the firm had not attracted people of the right calibre, nor had it projected future demand for managers. As a result, it soon had difficulty finding people of management potential from the present staff.

To help solve the problem, a keen training officer was hired to set up what he called a management-trainee scheme. Merrily, he recruited young men with college educations, promised them early appointments as store managers, and invested a lot of effort and money in their training. After two years, these trainees were ready for their first management appointments. Unfortunately, the results did not work out very well. During those few years, the pattern of retailing had begun to change: small shops were giving

77

way to larger, self-service stores; bigger shopping centres serving wider areas were being opened and the firm was now faced with redundant managers. Any talk of appointing the newly prepared trainees to management positions brought a swift and hostile reaction from existing managers, and the scheme understandably crumbled.

This example provides both a case for management development and a case against it. At first, the firm had a problem because it did not plan for the future; then it had a problem because it did.

There is always a case for and against future planning. The case for is based on three main arguments.

1. Future planning can help identify likely 'people gaps' in the future. This knowledge will allow the time and effort necessary to train and develop employees.
2. It helps sort out who, within the firm, can be developed to a higher position. It is nonsense to develop people without a clear view of what they are being developed for and, if you are not careful, you could find yourself developing people for your competitors.
3. If people know they have a good future with you, they are more likely to stay.

The case against future planning is based on two principal arguments.

1. It can lead to decisions being made too far ahead of time, like the firm mentioned earlier. Thus, if the situation changes, you could be left committed to the wrong horse.
2. By saying who is likely to get ahead in your firm, you are also, by default, saying who is likely to remain at the same level. Almost nothing turns people off faster than letting them know that they have no future.

Learning continually has to take place at the organizational, team and individual levels. One of the most serious and frequent organizational problems is a lack of management learning. For example, in 1980 the top management team of the Caterpillar Company was congratulating itself on its greatest ever profit performance. Despite its festival of self-congratulation the harbingers of corporate disaster were hovering nearby. Changing patterns of world trade, an economic downturn and inflated costs were about to wound Caterpillar and cost hundreds of millions of dollars over the next five years. Why were the top managers of this great company apparently oblivious to the impending crisis? The answer appears to lie in a false but collective perception of reality held by the chief executive and his top team who were justifiably proud of their decades of outstanding achievement and failed to learn that the nature of the world's earthmoving equipment industry was undergoing a profound change.

It is vital that the top team in an organization learns from the environment. Many significant changes can occur which need to be detected, understood and categorized as opportunities or threats. A dominant chief executive who is closed to learning is especially dangerous. The training of the upper strata of managers is the single most potent act that can be taken to develop an organization as a learning system. Top managers need highly developed skills in these ten areas:

- industry analysis
- competitor analysis
- organizational appraisal
- forming corporate identity
- competitive strategies
- implementation tactics
- effective management processes
- sustaining a healthy climate
- persuasion techniques
- clarifying corporate values.

Management development activity must not be focused solely on the individual. Team development is a powerful training technique which has recently become better understood. Any spectator of a team game will tell you that brilliant individuals can fail to work well as a team. Co-ordinated effort requires more than individual skills - relationships between team members make all the difference.

Every good organization needs to identify competences associated with success and to provide development processes which build these capabilities. Competence must be objectively analysed. It is related to performance in specific roles. Playing the oboe in an orchestra clearly requires different competences from those of an effective chief executive.

Competence is the capacity to perform reliably to an acceptable standard. A simple analogy helps to explain the concept. You, the reader, can probably drive a car. At the moment you are reading, and not (hopefully) driving. Yet you have the intellectual, emotional and physical skills, knowledge, attitude, perceptual sharpness and willingness to drive. You possess everything needed to sit behind the wheel and be fully responsible for the vehicle. You are a 'competent' driver.

The competence concept has five components:

- skill: being able to perform, in the correct sequence, difficult or complex techniques
- knowledge: having relevant data, helpfully organized, and being able to use an appropriate body of knowledge
- attitude: constructive emotional stance and willingness to perform to a high standard
- self-concept: confidence in one's ability to achieve
- perceptual sharpness: being able to pay attention to things that matter in doing a good job.

All five components interact. Knowledge is needed for skill, which guides perception, which shapes attitude and so on. Imagine it as a spider's web: thinking, feeling and performing all support each other to provide competence.

All roles demand a number of specific competences. Consider a driver again. He or she must drive the car safely, deal with minor mechanical emergencies, insure it and so on. Each of these activities makes different demands and requires distinct competences. It is helpful to specify them for assessment and training. When you are driving in traffic correct road-positioning and judging road conditions will need to be looked at separately.

Competence analysis is a superb practical tool. Begin by studying the people who succeed in the role at present. Ask: What are their strengths? How do they approach their roles? What techniques do they use? How do they spend their time? When you have clearly identified the competences of those performing the job you desire, examine your managers' capacities and ask: Where are they lacking?

There are no competences which apply to all jobs; the management developer must identify those that are necessary and, especially, those that result in excellence. It is foolish to rely on conventional wisdom about what distinguishes those who are successful. We should define only relevant skills, knowledge, attitudes and self-concept factors, identifying them by assiduous observation.

Career transitions mean not only that new competences must be acquired; redundant ones must be dropped. The successful salesman is probably energetic, pushy and outgoing, but sales managers need a different set of competences in order to perform well; for example, they're likely to be excellent motivators and planners. In fact, some of the competences which are essential at junior levels are unhelpful for more senior roles.

The management developer is well advised to undertake this process:

- Categorize managers into 'unsuccessful' and 'successful' performers.
- Study both unsuccessful and successful performers (be objective: use tests).
- Find out exactly what both low and high performers do.
- Ask what sort of behaviour contributes to success.
- Carefully list the behaviour traits in writing – do not jump to conclusions.
- Compare 'best' with 'worst'. What are the differences?
- Go outside your own organization and look at successful performers in the roles to validate your conclusions.
- Check textbooks, autobiographies etc. to give different perspectives.
- Write a detailed description of the necessary competences in the wanted role which result in high performance.
- Compare this with current capabilities and prepare an action plan to fill gaps.

Managers should be placed in situations where they are forced to develop competences which they lack. This approach to development is known as 'action learning' and works on the principle that people learn best by doing, not by contemplating. In addition, managers need a 'mentor', who is a guide, supporter, counsellor, disciplinarian and patron. The mentor should know what competences are needed and should create opportunities to enable them to be acquired.

A close relationship develops; mentors must get to know each individual.

Mentoring itself requires special competences to help people face reality and know their weaknesses and strengths. The mentor should become an expert in giving feedback which is realistic, evaluative and positive. He or she helps the individual perceive and conceptualize in new ways, and assists in reorganizing experiences and identifying key points. Under mentoring and action learning, new competences are acquired, including informal and political ones.

However, competences alone may not be enough. 'Being' is important. This means enhancing maturity, depth, inner resourcefulness and stature. The path we tread in the world, despite all vicissitudes, is a statement of who we are and what we believe to be important. It isn't surprising that some religious traditions see a direct connection between spiritual and worldly development. Hermann Hesse's book *Siddhartha*[1] describes how mystical insights learned in the wilderness during a spiritual quest later enabled the hero to achieve great worldly success.

If depth of character is related to achievement, then logic tells us that management development is incomplete without an element of personal search. Those who achieve high office are clear about their beliefs and values; on the whole they have well-developed personal attributes. Self-knowledge makes a significant contribution to personal energy.

Personal growth comes from the individual, not from the environment. It requires a degree of autonomy, which is often discouraged by formal education systems.

Managers in today's world need to be competent in the following eleven areas:

1. *Self-management competence.* Management is a demanding task, often sapping mental and emotional energy. The competent manager has a deep understanding of time management and keeps fit in every sense of the word.
2. *Clear values.* Managers have to take decisions on what is more or less worthwhile. Such choices should be based on defensible values. The competent manager has clear, consistent, tested values which are felt to be right.
3. *Clear goals.* Management is about getting things done despite difficulties. This requires the capacity to focus resources on

defined end results. The competent manager sets realistic, measurable and challenging goals.

4. Continuous personal development. The pace of development is so rapid that managers rapidly become obsolete if their competence does not continue to evolve. People need to take responsibility for managing their own development. The competent manager deliberately takes steps to grow as a person, and as a manager, throughout life.

5. Problem-solving skills. Things going wrong are the daily grind of management. Solutions to non-routine, complex or ambiguous issues must be found. The competent manager is a skilful and methodical problem solver.

6. High creativity. Machines increasingly perform routine tasks but managers have to deal with novel challenges. This requires both personal creativity and the ability to channel the talents of others. The competent manager is able to rise above convention, thereby finding new opportunities and solutions to intractable problems.

7. High influence. The capacity to persuade others is essential. Scarce resources need to be acquired, and influential people won over. Such skills as effective assertion, capable negotiating and persuasive argument are relevant. The competent manager is an effective influence on others – upwards, sideways and below.

8. Managerial insight. Creating the right climate for people to give their best requires insightful management. This includes selecting appropriate management styles and motivating others. The competent manager creates an open and positive climate which gives people the support and direction that they need.

9. High supervisory skills. Much management time is spent juggling resources and reallocating priorities. Organizations must be built, systems constructed and controls established. The competent manager is a master of supervision.

10. Trainer capacity. The success of a manager is measured by the efficiency of the unit which he or she controls. This means that continuous development of the skills of subordinates is needed. This may be achieved through appraisal, giving feedback, coaching, counselling or direct training. The competent manager develops the potential of others.

11. Team-building skills. People like to work with others. Teamwork is important for both motivational and practical reasons. Often complex objectives can be achieved only through team effort. The competent manager is an effective teambuilder.

A fuller explanation of these eleven competences can be found in *The Unblocked Manager,* a book written by us and published by Gower in 1982.

Training a management group requires attention to each of these eleven areas. Competence is primarily developed in the real world. Managers can be helped by education, training and coaching but they need to be put in situations where they have to achieve optimum results in the untidy world of daily reality – where pressures, illogicalities and resource shortages are ever present. Increasingly we realize that a capable management is a source of sustainable competitive advantage.

Key concepts

- Development of individual potential is an important contributor to organizational success
- Although long-term planning has some inherent weaknesses, there is no alternative to planning the development of managerial ability
- The skills of top managers in particular are crucial to organizational success
- Top managers need to be developed as a team
- The competence approach helps to clarify management development needs
- Competences include skills, knowledge, attitudes, self-concept and perceptual sharpness
- The competences needed for specific roles should be objectively identified
- Action learning is an effective approach to managerial development
- Managers need skilled mentors as guides
- Eleven generic competences can be identified: self-management competence, clear values, clear goals, continuous personal development, problem-solving skills, high creativity, high influence, managerial insight, high supervisory skills, trainer capacity and team-building skills
- A capable management team is seen as a source of sustainable competitive advantage.

Reference

1. Hermann Hesse, *Siddhartha*, Bantam, New York, 1982.

Blockage 5 – Confused organizational structure

'Insight without action breeds anxiety.
Action without insight breeds confusion.'
Inspired by Barry A. Goodfield

No matter how businesses are organized, people will probably complain that the total effect is frustrating, and often inefficient. Yet, despite all the difficulties, organizations are necessary features of our society. They are our friends, and we need to know their strengths and weaknesses and to learn how to make them serve us. The organization should suit the needs of the business, not the reverse.

Whenever people are grouped together there are the inevitable problems of coordinating effort. As firms grow in size, the question of organization becomes more involved and more important – one that demands careful thought; otherwise, the difficulties of getting things done become so great that people are liable to give up trying and just concentrate on keeping out of trouble.

The simplest type of business is a single trader. Consider for example, a dealer in firewood. Every morning he collects wood, carries it to his house, chops it, and travels through town knocking on doors selling it. Suppose business booms and he decides to take on some extra help. He must then decide who chops, who collects the wood, who sells it, and how the different activities relate. In the early days, there will be few headaches over organization but, as the business expands, the woodcutter will have to learn how to delegate, a function many managers find difficult. As a small business grows, so does the need to have an appropriate structure.

Organizing is one of the problems that nag top management the most and it is never easy. It helps to understand the underlying principles. Some of the basic concepts were first described in the eighteenth century. Who does what or who controls what is probably the biggest cause of rows, recriminations and undercover fighting. A person building a business often has so many painful experiences that he believes the only one he can trust is himself and that other people are either too limited or unreliable.

Adam Smith, one of the first observers of the effects of industrialization on patterns of work, made his classic study of a group of pin-makers. He explained that, using division of labour, the group's output was vastly greater than a similar number of isolated people completing all of the tasks themselves. Division of labour is a key to efficiency, but creates a need to ensure that people work together to achieve the desired overall results.

Consider a straightforward example. College lecturers are all specialists: one in industrial law, another in taxation accounting, a third in management policy and so on. Students require an integrated course, so college lecturers must coordinate their work together. Mechanisms for doing this include timetables, syllabuses, meetings, policy statements, informal contact and managerial responsibility. In more complex environments, like the armed services at war, a phenomenal amount of communication is necessary in order to orchestrate many different resources. In fact, the need for integration varies according to the size of the organization and the tasks undertaken.

The degree of precision and complexity required by the task is variable. A jazz band relies on the players being alert to each other and constantly adjusting their music in the general direction of the tune. A similarly sized musical group, a string quartet, has a more precise task and depends on careful adherence to a musical score (which is the primary integrating mechanism) to perform a Mozart piece. A large organization with a precise and complex task, like a symphony orchestra, requires more managerial integration and so defers to the direction of a conductor.

Large organizations are essential to perform complex tasks (like mass-producing motor cars) or benefiting from economies of scale (like oil refining). They have five distinct specializations:

1. Operators who do the work.
2. Managers who direct, control and co-ordinate.
3. Analysts who innovate, standardize and rationalize processes.
4. Support staff who enable work to proceed.
5. Directors who establish the direction of the organization, make key decisions and monitor performance.

Complex systems are developed by analysts and implemented by middle managers. Top management has the task of making important decisions, allocating resources and evaluating performance. Operators have the simple task of performing their specified roles. Managers struggle with many complexities as they turn objectives into action programmes.

Simplification is often impossible and communication systems become extremely elaborate. Consider a production department making small batches of complex equipment which require hundreds of parts, each ordered from specialist suppliers with varying lead times. Tens of thousands of interdependent movements take place in a typical week. Meanwhile, in the development department bright engineers are changing designs, then changing the specification. Production workers swap parts to meet urgent needs and confuse the record keepers. All this adds to the complexity. Economic considerations compel cost-conscious managers to seek reductions in expensive stocks and keep investment to a minimum. Over-ordering, the easy way of dealing with such problems, is unacceptable. Managers faced with such problems develop techniques for controlling the situation, even developing a special language with precise concepts like 'tentative stock orders', 'stock simulation reports', 'sequencing protocols', and 'change concessions'. Such concepts are essential mechanisms for integration even though they may appear an esoteric mystique of specialists.

The mushrooming complexity in large organizations can only be dealt with by systems and specialization. Computer control of complex systems permits a level of integration previously impossible. Man could not journey to the moon until computers became available. Unfortunately the interdependence of elements increases the need for the whole system to work at levels of effectiveness previously unachieved. Massive breakdowns with horrendous complications become more possible. The risks of failure are catastrophic, so considerable investment in sustaining effective integration despite equipment malfunction is essential.

Organizational types

An effective organization is both specialised and integrated. How can managers tackle the essential task of choosing the best organization? It is now widely understood that the question, 'What is the best way to organize?' has only one valid answer: 'It depends on what you want to organize'. Knowledge about the best ways to organize enables managers to make judgements on the basis of expertise, as a surgeon, rather than hunches and experience, like a magician.

Functional structures develop excellence in technical specialisms but tend to be poor in integrating the work of different functions. Product-based structures often have the opposite weakness: they fail to sustain real specialist capability. We need some way of defining particular organizational types. This is an important but somewhat complex topic and we acknowledge that much of the following discussion is based on the brilliant work of Professor Mintzberg.[1]

Following his analysis, there are five distinct types of organization. We will consider each, briefly describe its characteristics, and consider the implications for organizational design.

Simple structure

This is a small (or crisis-ridden) organization, often in its pioneer stage, ruled by one or two people. It is controlled by direct supervision of the boss. Often a family firm, the simple structure is flexible, unformalized and autocratic. Many small businesses (or organizations in crisis) thrive under clear 'hands-on' leadership by a boss. Complexity, excess staff, over-elaborate systems and formality are enemies. The boss takes decisions, seizes opportunities and aggressively confronts the world. But beware! The simple structure is the most risky of all, as it depends on the health and drive of one person. Also, expansion is limited, since the lack of formal organization prevents large tasks from being managed.

The simple structure requires that the boss knows every key employee. Information is conveyed to the boss, who is the hub of the wheel – in the centre of everything. It is imperative that the centralized decision taker knows precisely what is going on. Flexibility and decisiveness are essential as is a sense of mission. The boss is the only person who can convey direction and objectives to the workforce.

Machine bureaucracy

This is an organization based on rules, procedures, systems and controls. It is controlled by precise specification of work processes. As far as possible, people are used as interchangeable elements in complex systems, trained to behave like cogs in a well-oiled wheel. Organizations, like airlines or post offices, have many routine tasks to perform predictably time and time again. Tasks become highly specialized. Rules and regulations abound. Communication is formalized and elaborate. Different functions have their own managers who are expert in their discipline. Specialists, like work study analysts, accountants, quality controllers and planners proliferate. Without them the organization would collapse into inefficient chaos. Managers are 'obsessed with control', seeking to measure all variables and eliminate uncertainties.

Although the machine bureaucracy is technically efficient, there are latent conflicts which threaten productivity. Controls and disciplines are dehumanizing and tensions mount. Often management can only ameliorate or bottle up potential trouble.

Managers must develop sophisticated systems to collect data, monitor performance and set up systems of rules and procedures. Discipline is all important. The manager in a machine bureaucracy must communicate formal systems and disciplines in ways which ordinary people will accept. Transgressions must be dealt with effectively. Enlightened managements in such organizations do what they can to help people find meaning in their work. Although the character of the organization diminishes motivation, effective communication can mitigate some of the harmful effects of treating people like machines.

Professional bureaucracy

This is an organization where the most important work is carried out by professionals. It is controlled by selecting and training competent individuals. A hospital is a good example. The organization supports the work of professional doctors and surgeons. Police forces, universities, hospitals and accounting firms all require highly-skilled individuals able to meet complex but predictable requirements. There is much delegation of decision making.

This type of organization is dependent on the competence of skilled workers who must be trusted to do the job in a professional way. All doctors are expected to make a thorough diagnosis when a patient arrives with a complaint, but the subsequent treatment varies from patient to patient. Doctors cannot be supervised or programmed all the time – that would be vastly expensive and counter-productive – so the organization provides an environment which sets basic standards and then enables highly-trained professionals to get on with their work. In professional bureaucracies there is an enormous amount of training and education. Professional skills and attitudes take years to accumulate and must be regularly updated.

Those in management roles have to avoid simplistic rule-making or its opposite, abdication. They need to develop a steering and co-ordinating role. Power is largely decentralized and managerial leadership is persuasive rather than autocratic. For this reason it is difficult to determine corporate strategy.

Although professional bureaucracies provide deeply satisfying work for individuals, the lack of a strong central organization means that decision making emerges from political intrigue. Influence rather than reason may rule the day. Also, independent professionals sometimes abuse their position by laziness or unethical conduct. Innovation, which requires the co-operation of colleagues, is notoriously difficult to orchestrate. In fact, creative thinking often fails to flourish as such organizations work along time-proven lines. The difficulty of obtaining the willing co-operation of many independent people means that change proceeds with almost painful slowness. It is difficult to manage by objectives since outputs are intangible. However, despite all of the disadvantages, organizations which ask people to perform varied and complex tasks have no option but to place control in the hands of the operator. Nothing else has been proven to work.

Divisionalized form

This is a large organization which has divided operations into manageable units. Each division is controlled by careful measurement of outputs. Divisions become the operating units, each serving a distinct market. As each division is largely independent, much authority and responsibility are delegated to divisional management teams. Most large profit-making organizations since the Second World War have evolved specialized divisions to suit particular markets. The divisionalized form pushes decision making downwards and duplicates functions – every division has a full complement of analysts and experts. It is expensive in overheads but allows units to be profit centres and independently measureable. Headquarters allow much freedom but carefully monitor results. Much day-by-day authority is given to unit managers whose skills are critical, so training and indoctrination are vital to ensure consistently high-quality decision making.

Divisions develop their own goals and negotiate with headquarters. Quantitative measures are required; without them control cannot be exercised. A sympathetic use of both carrot and stick best describes the relationship between headquarters and division. Headquarters maintain control over strategic planning, allocate financial resources, establish control systems, appoint key personnel, conduct basic research and form broad policies. The divisions focus attention on markets they know and are able to be decisive.

The divisionalized form is one solution to a problem of red tape. Huge monolithic bureaucracies, structured like spiders' webs, are ponderous, stultifying and maladaptive. The divisionalized form of organization enables people to thrive and take initiatives to succeed (or not) on the basis of their own efforts.

The divisionalized form of structure has its costs. Sometimes units devote scarce resources repeating work which another part of the organization has already undertaken; or large projects requiring economies of scale are not undertaken because people 'think small'. The divisionalized form has the following negative characteristics:

- divisional management tends to develop protective mechanisms against headquarters
- divisions tend to become exclusive and not share objectives with sister units
- overall strategy is difficult to convey as divisions are concerned with the threats and opportunities of the moment
- much communication with headquarters is formalized, dealing with financial information, which means that top management can be out of touch.

Adhocracy

This is an organization which operates in a complex and turbulent world where innovation is essential. It is controlled by discussion between experts. Rigid organizations are incapable of giving the flexibility which is necessary for a high level of creativity. Accordingly, an organization is called for which is organic and changes shape according to current needs. The solution is an adhocracy. Bureaucracy is consciously avoided. Teams tackle particular projects and then disband. Individuals are encouraged to follow their own interests. A great amount of co-ordination is necessary to derive something productive from the melée of creative activity.

If the task is to build a new generation computer, manufacture prototypes or manage a rock group then throw away the formal options and devise an adhocracy. This requires breaking away from established patterns, and not relying on standardization or formalization which would stifle creativity. Adhocracies should be open with frequent meetings and frequent reviews. Clear job demarcations, invariable routines and rigid disciplines are unhelpful. All manner of techniques are vital to co-ordinate work. Change is often needed. In the first eight years of its life, the American NASA organization changed its structure seventeen times. As bureaucracy increased in NASA it became vulnerable to defective decision making.

Adhocracies grow complex and untidy – often using the two-boss matrix concept – yet such structural untidiness is essential to their innovative power. Managers develop skills in handling bewildering and divergent situations. They become expert co-ordinators and resource allocators. Power is held by those who have expertise rather than formal bosses. Top management has the role of accumulating resources and reassigning specialists to the needs of the moment. Strategy is reviewed many times as new facts emerge. Action planning from the top may impede achievement because only the originators of projects know enough to get them done. Top managers spend much time identifying strategic options and deciding between highly complex arguments. They try to control, but often can only intervene after the event when the money has already been spent.

Some of the most innovative firms are adhocracies. Two examples are Bell Laboratories in the United States and Sinclair Research Limited in England, both of which designed world-beating products. Such organizations tend to be most dramatically creative in their youth but, as we all know, youth is a time of high energy but suspect decision making.

Culture

The organization of a firm is the result of thousands of decisions made by the people who work there. Yet once precedents become established and the attitudes of influential people become enshrined as the company's spirit or 'culture' people rarely take a step back and ask whether the firm's basic beliefs and assumptions are still valid or morally right.

That people differ widely in their attitudes towards authority is an important aspect. Perhaps the most common difference is between those who wish to keep authority and control with the boss (autocratic style) and those who want to distribute authority and control more widely (participative style). Although both methods have worked well in some situations and have failed in others, it is most important to achieve an organizational and managerial style that fits the needs of the situation at a particular time. Today, many organizational leaders feel that they need to shift away from autocracy towards more participative management approaches.

Autocratic style

In the autocratic approach, which centralizes control, decisions can be made quickly and uniformity is insured. Employees, however, have little or no influence in decision making. This system of management has many levels, clear job demarcations, and defined procedures. The boss holds the strings, writes the lines, and directs the play. Others do not get a chance to influence events. Some people, who dislike responsibilities, enjoy this, but many get angry and depressed under an authoritarian regime. This is especially true when the man or woman at the centre is incompetent or inhumane. It is one thing to be led by a person of wisdom, humanity and purpose; it is quite another to be ruled by someone with the qualities of stupidity and bungling ineptitude.

In a situation where there is a very strong, autocratic boss, subordinates do not get a chance to develop and, as a result, they often acquire the servile mentality of a schoolboy in a Dickens novel.

Participative style

The participative approach is a more difficult management philosophy to practise, yet it has been associated with many high-performing organizations throughout the world. Perhaps the most common characteristics are that each person is involved in matters that affect him and that the organization cares about individuals' needs.

On the positive side, the participative style of management can lead to increased motivation and communication, while encouraging a team approach to common tasks. On the other hand, it can create more problems because a wider distribution of views is taken into account, which may result in excuses for inaction, vacillation, and confusion.

It has been said that the best place to make decisions is where the problem hurts. However, unless there is an organization-wide perspective on team building, work groups may satisfy their own needs rather than those of the organization.

Appropriate organization structure and culture

In the 1930s, writers on management produced dozens of books advising managers how to organize. Their concepts read like a search for the pot of gold at the end of the rainbow. The pundits believed a secret principle existed that, once discovered, would yield an orderly, invincible and profitable formula for building a perfect business machine. Unfortunately the search was misguided and the single ideal organization proved a myth. Through research, however, more systematic ways have been found to get a good 'fit' between the managment structure and the technology of a firm.

The desired situation in an organization is for the division of labour to be the best possible compromise between the jobs that have to be done (technology) and the desire of people who work there to have satisfying and meaningful jobs. There should also be sufficient flexibility within the structure to adapt to changing situations, and a way of helping people develop for their future. An appropriate organization structure is like a fit body: each function contributes individually and the whole is well coordinated.

Symptoms of inappropriate organization

An inappropriate structure is a very costly ailment that can result in the organization firing on four cylinders out of six. Functions that are unimportant or even irrelevant can grow out of proportion when a powerful, self-seeking manager creates a vast empire that is nothing more than a monument to himself. The appearance of such an organization resembles a beer drinker whose body is in poor shape but whose right arm is well muscled from lifting endless glasses of beer.

Issues are often left unresolved. Most companies have at least one poor performer who has been moved to a niche where, hopefully, not too much damage will result. Often he has had a managerial job, but because he no longer has the perseverance, energy or imagination to do that job successfully and because the organization thinks it owes him some kind of debt, he is put out to grass, perhaps in the personnel department. There he sits bungling or blocking every useful idea that comes his way. A first test of a company that wants to improve its organization is to face issues like this in a strong but humane way.

Another familiar symptom of bad organization is that some jobs are not accomplished at all. We know of one company that put a lot of energy into efficiently transporting materials two hundred miles for processing. Because no one was responsible for considering whether it would be cheaper to close the distant plant and to build an extension to the home factory, this situation lasted for eight years before anyone was made aware of the wasted energy involved.

There are widespread views on the merits of job descriptions ranging from 'a necessity for any job' to 'a straitjacket that stifles initiative'. Again, it is necessary to ask where you stand and whether any job-definition problems, such as the following, affect your firm. Does management have difficulty deciding on real priorities? Does management waste time doing unnecessary things? Do you have doubts about the necessity of some jobs? Is achievement sometimes measured unrealistically? Are there 'who-does-what' disputes?

Organization is a very subtle and confusing subject, one that needs to be watched carefully. A structure that is completely appropriate and alive today may become unsatisfactory and dead in a few months or years. But there are no magic formulas, and another company's organization can never be completely appropriate to your own situation. Therefore, the objective is to form a structure that suits your own particular circumstances, which may involve difficult choices between opposites every step of the way.

The organization of a firm is a living network of communication, discussion, consultation and decision making. When it works well, an infinitely larger quantity of human potential is put to constructive use. Organization is about people's lives.

Key concepts

• The complexity of organizations increases with size and growth

- Large organizations usually have five distinct specializations – operators, managers, analysts, support staff and directors
- Division of labour is a key to efficiency
- Five main types of organization can be identified
- The simple structure is centralized and organic
- The machine bureaucracy is formalized and co-ordinated by systems and routines
- The professional bureaucracy provides a complex service so power moves to the operators
- The divisionalized form organizes to address specific markets
- The adhocracy is creative and frequently reorganizing
- Organization culture defines how structures function
- Participative structures, despite their difficulties, are increasingly associated with high performing organizations
- When organization structure is appropriate more human potential is realized
- Organization is about people's lives.

Reference

1. Henry Mintzberg, *Structuring in Fives,* Prentice-Hall, Englewood Cliffs, New Jersey, 1983.

Blockage 6 – Inadequate control

> 'I think one must finally take
> one's life in one's arms'.
> Arthur Miller

We have two friends with very similar business problems. One built up a very successful manufacturing company. He owned a couple of Mercedes, a large yacht and every other conceivable comfort, but he did not really enjoy them because he was a worried man. You could almost see his hairs turning grey, one by one, as you talked to him. As he put it; 'Things are going wrong in my business and I don't know where to kick'. Although parts of his company were doing well, others were spoiling the picture, and he did not know which functions were causing the problems.

Our second friend was sitting in his office one morning feeling very cheerful because his balance sheet for the previous financial year showed an excellent profit. Now you might assume that he had nothing to be concerned about, but the profit worried him because it came as a complete surprise, and it would have been no more surprising if the profit had been a loss.

Both our friends had control problems. They ran successful companies but they were not in control of what was happening.

Control problems usually start to plague a business when it is expanding. In the early stages of a firm's development the owner is intimately concerned with all aspects of everyday business life. As the firm grows, he or she must accept the fact that he can no longer make all the decisions. Many owners of businesses have real difficulty accepting this and cling to the traditional tasks they have always performed. We know of one highly successful senior manager who still insists on opening and locking his factory door each day. The consequences of such managerial gluttony can easily lead to incompetence or a nervous breakdown.

At the other extreme is the manager who delegates everything, even the really crucial things, without maintaining any form of control over what has been delegated.

As a business expands it becomes imperative to develop systems of control that will largely look after themselves. Many businesses have floundered into confusion, gloom, hysteria, and eventually bankruptcy because they lacked basic control procedures.

Effective control

Effective control is related to the five organizational types described in Blockage 5.

In the 'simple structure' excessive formality is rarely seen. One of the authors remembers establishing his first small business some years ago. When the time came to submit the annual accounts the unsorted receipts were in shoeboxes, and it was only with the tolerant help of a systematic friend that the accounts could be prepared. Red tape was totally absent! Even rudimentary systems were lacking; the embryonic business needed formality and bureaucracy. Later, a new employee joined the team and she insisted on strict procedures which were welcomed as saviours.

This example is typical. Most simple structures are not elaborate because the founder could operate with minimal administrative machinery. Should the enterprise grow, or the founder move on, then successors are less likely to be able to manage by the seats of their pants.

Formal control in simple structures tends to be underdeveloped. It is likely that information is neither collected nor processed efficiently. The boss often fails to use systematic administrative systems or up-to-date technology. Progress, sometimes survival, requires formality and discipline.

In the 'machine bureaucracy' there is a very different situation. Here everything is documented. An international electronics company has a manual of procedures which includes telling staff what kinds of wine to buy for customers' lunches, and specifies the exact typeface to be used on overhead projector slides.

Control is exercised through specification of processes and so the technical quality of controls is paramount. The Jaguar story provides a useful illustration. The chief executive, John Egan, had a virtually bankrupt company when he took over in 1980. He used a scythe to cut out excess resources. Interestingly, not everywhere was cut; Egan hired more people in the engineering function. He argued that high quality engineering surveillance was essential to ensure well-built cars. Jaguar needed better standardization.

In poorly managed machine bureaucracies, red tape stimulates growth in informal communication or 'grapevines'. Unresponsive and unwieldy systems are circumvented by backdoor arrangements. People get their information through personal contacts. There is fertile ground for politics and nepotism to thrive. The informal system, however, is not always counter-productive. Ironically, some of the most valuable initiatives are taken outside official channels.

Ill-conceived or poorly managed administration dampens enthusiasm and strangles initiative. People become part of a system, functioning in a cosy world of forms, procedures, reports and protocols. Nothing is urgent or special. So there is no possibility of exploiting the creative power of anxiety and the value of desperation. At first sight, emotion may seem counter-productive, but consider the situation of a chief executive who finds his products nearing the end of their life-cycle and has no ready substitutes. Top management is pressurizing by asking questions. Perhaps the shareholders or banks begin to withdraw support. The workforce is showing anxieties. Trade union representatives detect potential problems and blame the management. Scare stories in the local newspaper may add to the pressure. Alarm, insecurity, anxiety and naked fear are present. Emotions communicate more than the words. Urgency, by itself, can be blind and lead to panic. But, when structured, it excites enthusiasm, releases initiative and cuts through red tape.

The 'professional bureaucracy' is different again. In schools, universities, agencies and hospitals it is difficult to find out what is going on. Watching a hospital at work gives vivid illustration. Each doctor has a batch of patients, loosely organized by the type of ailment they suffer from. However, in one case, one patient had three malaises – earache, a kidney disorder and a skin rash. Despite strenuous efforts by the senior nursing officer, it proved impossible to get the ENT surgeon, kidney specialist and dermatologist together to provide an integrated programme of care for the unfortunate patient. Power is decentralized in professional bureaucracies.

The difficulty that the patient with three ailments experiences is that power is in the hands of professionals who specialize in treating only one part of the body. The ENT surgeon is as uninterested in the patient's skin as a florist would be in the contents of a fishmonger's shop. Because patients have both ears and skin the medical distinctions cannot really remain separate. Effective control integrates the work of specialists. This is difficult to orchestrate while each specialist concentrates on a narrow expertise.

Individual professionals must be allowed to exercise their skills within an overall vision of the future which integrates the work of everyone in the professional bureaucracy. Inevitably, power is shared. The essence of high-performing professional bureaucracies is sustaining balance between the needs of the organization and the professionals who make it work.

The fourth type of organization, the 'divisionalized form' was devised as an elegant administrative solution to the potential problem of over-centralized decision taking. Most of the illustrations are from the world of commerce but, for variety, consider a military case study. At its height the Roman Empire had such countries as England, Egypt and much of what is now the Soviet Union within its 6,000-mile border. In the second century, Rome was able to control some 50 million people with an army of just 300,000 well equipped and superbly trained soldiers. Their military strategy was based on key fortresses along the frontiers. As the border was threatened local commanders had all the resources to deal with the situation themselves. Later, in the third century, the policy was reversed and the centre became the heart of military might. The abandonment of the divisionalized structure was one of the factors that led to the downfall of the Roman Empire in 476 AD.

The jargon of today tells us that the Roman Empire operated as a divisionalized form during its most successful years. Strong local commanders took total responsibility for their regions and

Rome exercised overall strategic control. There was a clear separation of duties between the Emperor and the fortress commandants. Effective control was encouraged by well-defined limits of authority.

However, central leaderships faltered as emperors pursued their licentious and drunken debauches rather than settling down to strategic planning conferences. The empire began to fall apart. Power was taken from the divisional commanders and given to crazed and ignorant hedonistic sots. Nero fiddled while Rome burned. The integrity of the organizational concept was destroyed and Rome declined and fell.

In the divisionalized form of organization it is vital that accurate information on performance is rapidly processed upwards. Strategic decisions require an enormous amount of data. These have to be collected and sifted, summarized and put into sensible formats. Such 'filters' need regular attention to ensure that they do their job properly. This is especially difficult to manage in decentralized organizations.

Despite the difficulties of strategic decision taking, when there is a developed command, control and intelligence system, the divisionalized form is essential to managing organizations today. It permits a focus on a particular product or market and can provide a nice balance between centralized control and autonomy.

The last form of organization is the 'adhocracy'. This buzzing and creative melee of frequently changing structures is again best illustrated by an example. One of us was asked to work as a consultant to an ad hoc team whose task was to design a common chassis for a wide range of electric and gas cookers. All the relevant experts were assembled, bright engineers, designers, production experts, planners and marketing specialists.

At the start there was no organization or role description. Everything had to be done from scratch. The team members had to get to know each other, set up a temporary organization, clarify objectives, agree a process of work and keep changing their organization over the busy weeks in which the new chassis design was devised. The creativity was infectious. One participant remarked: 'I know the goal but who the hell knows what's going to happen next? The synergy is fantastic. Meetings are constantly being called, and each one changes something important. The process is unpredictable. Really exciting.'

Adhocracies are destroyed by rigid administrative frameworks. Systems, procedures, conventions and protocols all undermine the vigour of the adhocracy. People with expertise working informally together is the only way to make an adhocracy work.

The search for appropriate control

Each of these five organizational types needs different disciplines of control. The simple structure is often excessively dependent on one person and lacks useful systems. The machine bureaucracy must be tightly controlled but can become strangled by inappropriate regulation. Professional bureaucracies become excessively fragmented as power is captured by isolated individuals. The divisionalized form is measured on short-term performance and so becomes excessively preoccupied with immediate events to the detriment of the long-term health. Adhocracies are hotbeds of innovation, but notoriously difficult to control; they depend on excellent informal communication.

Each form of organization must conduct a search for a control system that is suitable, prompt and quick-witted, but the nature of the enemy varies in each case:

- in the simple structure it is a war against underdeveloped or immature systems
- in the machine bureaucracy it is a war against unintelligent systems
- in the professional bureaucracy it is a war against fragmented and repressive systems
- in the divisionalized form it is a war against short-term financial systems and head office interference
- in the adhocracy it is a war against rigid systems.

Direction implies control. A chief executive decides that all salesmen will wear white shirts and grey socks. A directive is issued, but is unlikely to be implemented unless the salesmen are controlled. Someone has to inspect their clothing and punish transgression. Control is a very important concept. In order to help us understand the relationship between direction and control we discuss the three types of control in more depth.

The first method of control is 'action planning'. This requires those with authority to plan what actions are needed and others are expected to play their part. When several fire crews attend a straightforward incident, the firemen look to their chief for instructions. Only he has the information to direct operations. The firemen do what they are told and integration is effected by a military-style chain of command.

Where the primary method of control is action planning, people need to know what should be done, what sequence to follow, how to perform the defined tasks and what to do if things go wrong. The required behaviours need to be specified to ensure a high standard of achievement. An almost mechanical adherence to procedures is sought.

The second method is 'performance control' where those with authority determine what results are needed, give objectives and then measure performance. Actions are not planned, as people are allowed to find their own ways to get things done. To illustrate the point, consider the firemen again. Suppose that the incident is not straightforward and a team must enter the smoke-filled building to find the heart of the fire. The fire chief will pick an experienced crew and instruct them: 'Get to the seat of the fire and try to put it out'. The team sets off with this objective, but no preformed action plan. It takes initiatives and develops action plans itself in the light of circumstances. The fire chief monitors performance. Integration is effected by management by objectives.

Where the primary method is performance control, participants must understand the required end results of their efforts. They need to be sure about the boundaries of their authority, the resources available, how they will be measured, and the relative priorities of different objectives. The required objectives are specified, but leave action planning to responsible individuals or teams.

The third method of control is 'policy enforcement' – policies are laid down which specify how people should behave. Our fire chief may believe that there are some children trapped in the burning building. A newspaper reporter approaches him and asks: 'What are the names of the children?' The fire chief mentally checks section 13, paragraph 18(b) of the procedure manual and replies: 'I cannot give you any personal details until the next of kin have been informed'. This is the fire service policy and the chief operates within it. Integration is effected through standardized application of policies and principles.

Where the primary method of control is policy enforcement, people need to understand the policies, rules, guidelines and conditions which circumscribe their work. In addition, they need to be able to categorize situations so that the 'correct' stance is taken. The meaning and the content of policies must be understood, and practitioners skilled at diagnosing when a particular policy is appropriate.

It is a principle of organization that action planning becomes less possible as unpredictability increases. The fire chief does not know what the crew will find as they work their way down smoke-filled corridors to the heart of the burning building. He could set an objective and establish policies, but not specify the actual behaviour required. Action planning provides the most comprehensive way to integrate the work of many people, but becomes counterproductive in uncertain situations.

Control is important to managers because their primary task is to decide what should be done and to ensure that the wanted results are achieved. Their basic decision is what form of control should they use – action planning and/or performance control and/or policy enforcement.

Lack of control

Although control is a complex subject, the symptoms of inadequate control are often quite obvious. An example is the manager who is unable to cope with all the demands on his time and who performs like a player in a speeded-up silent movie.

We know of one factory manager who had so many problems controlling his production that he never functioned correctly as an executive. You would often hear something like this in his factory:

> 'Joe, Unifoods has been on the phone again asking where its order is. You know we promised it by the 20th, so where the hell is it?'
> 'I'm sorry, Pete, but the stores were out of widgets again and by the time we got them, the assembly department was busy on that order for Smith.'

'Well, you're in charge of assembly, it's your job to sort it out. Why do you let this happen? You should arrange it ahead of time with the stores.'

'I don't run stores, you know, and sales shouldn't promise things without consulting us. Anyway, you are in charge, so it is your job to make sure everything is coordinated properly.'

'I haven't got ten pairs of hands, you know. I spend all my time sorting out shop floor problems now.'

Obviously, the production manager had a control problem, and he was at the centre of it. Even though everyone in the department knew problems existed, no one knew how to examine them carefully enough to prevent their reoccurring.

The remedy in this case was not an elaborate production-control system. All that was needed was a simple system that signalled a red light when a problem required attention - in this case, short and regular production meetings, during which any problems and issues were dealt with openly and targets and plans were laid for the following week.

Although the first few meetings were rather sordid, characterized by managers voicing old grievances, once all the 'dirt' was brought out into the open, reasons for shortcomings started to be discussed freely, and everyone began to find the meetings valuable. The senior man was better able to control what happened in the factory, and managers, instead of feeling tied down by targets and plans, saw the meetings as sources of help. The manager, instead of racing around the factory fire-fighting, was able to spend more of his time thinking and acting on the really important things that he used to neglect. As a result of the regular meetings, the reasons for variance from plans were examined and problems diminished in frequency.

Control belongs to management

One of the most important skills of professional management is to develop ways to bring order to complicated situations. Control is an inalienable management function; it cannot be subcontracted to an outside expert. However many instant solutions they read in books or hear in courses, managers must learn for themselves how to achieve and maintain control over their areas of responsibility, how to make up their own minds concerning what is 'too much' control and what is 'too little' control. Those who do not face these issues themselves become weaker and ineffective.

People are not machines

The control of machine performance is an engineering question, but with people, control is very much an emotional issue. Probably all of us, as children, experienced discipline and reacted against it at one time or another. If people are tied down by a control system that makes them feel stifled, at worst they will give up trying, and at best they will find some way of manipulating the system to their advantage. On the other hand, if they are treated responsibly and feel accountable for their own actions, they will see control as supportive and necessary.

A big problem with control is how perceptions and values appear in a different perspective when viewed from the management level and from the employee level. For example, something that appears to be entirely logical to the boss or to another department may be interpreted as unjust and ridiculous to the people lower in the organizational hierarchy who are affected by the decisions. One organization we know very well was once a small company where managers of the operating divisions controlled their own people without much interference from the head office. Because people worked largely on their own, the managers realized that any form of control needed to be supportive and not inhibitive. As one manager put it; 'If a guy is on his own for 90 per cent of his working life, then he really has to be responsible for his own actions'.

But soon the company expanded; three operating divisions turned into seven, and circumstances changed. Someone at the head office decided that more control was needed. Unfortunately, instead of working through the division managers, the head office tried to assume control by designing forms, instituting systems and issuing instructions. Soon thereafter, control began to be seen as inhibitive rather than supportive, and the staff began to wonder whether they were reporting to their own manager or some bureaucrat at the head office. The people at the head office did not understand the problems of operating the divisions, and their lack of knowledge showed in the paper work they designed. The managers of the operating divisions, incensed by the usurping of their own positions, felt that they were in conflict with head office and resorted to designing their own systems. Within six months, trade union membership in the operating divisions rose from 8 to 75 per cent, just one measure of how the workers felt about the situation. The people at the head office could not understand the resentment; as far as they were concerned, they were simply doing what was necessary and trying to be helpful.

Another friend of ours, who had all the trappings of a successful businessman, also illustrates how perceptions and values can change according to status and position. Usually he drove his luxurious sports car with an executive dash, but one day he needed to drive a five-ton truck. Much to his amazement, his whole attitude changed as he sat behind the driving wheel – he carved up private cars, show friendly courtesy to other commercial-vehicle drivers, and leered at passing girls. He was surprised that a change in his apparent position in society should have such an immediate effect on his behaviour.

Successful managers the world over acknowledge that one of their most important skills is knowing when to stand back, when to get involved, when to consult, when to make decisions and, perhaps most difficult of all, when to say 'yes' and 'no'. If a manager can detect trouble spots and keep control supportive he will be able to spend more time on other management functions. He will also avoid becoming chronically overloaded with unimportant details and gradually sinking into a morass of confusion as others watch with cynical amusement. Organizations are one of the most valuable resources known to man. They are the way in which human energy and ability can be directed towards the achievement of common goals. However, an organization without control is like a ship without a rudder. It is at the mercy of the elements and is likely to founder on the first rock which lies in its path.

Key concepts

- All organizations have problems of control
- In simple structures control is dependent on the competence of the boss
- In machine bureaucracies control is dependent on the excellence of systems
- In professional bureaucracies control must be delegated to the specialist
- In the divisionalized form of organization control is best exercised by the monitoring of performance
- In the adhocracy control is regulated by teams
- There are three basic forms of control: action planning, performance control and policy enforcement
- Managers must take control – there is no alternative
- Control should not be exercised in ways which diminish people's self-esteem
- Perceptions vary but are assumed to be valid by the holder
- Ultimate control belongs to management, it cannot be 'subcontracted' out.

Blockage 7 – Inadequate recruitment and selection

> 'Experience is the name
> every one gives to their
> mistakes.'
> Oscar Wilde

We know of a small company that sells highly specialized machinery to food manufacturers. It is famous for innovation and advanced design, and the management team recognizes that the company's greatest asset is the talent and creative skill of its research and development department.

Several years ago, the company needed to hire a new head of research and development. Because the job was vital to the wellbeing of the firm, senior managers held many conferences to determine who should be appointed. The production manager put it this way: 'If we make a bad decision this time, it will be like digging a big hole and jumping in'.

Because it is widely believed that outside people are somehow more capable and resourceful than those already in the organization, the management decided that none of the scientists working in the department possessed the necessary qualities to become manager. So the vacant post was advertised. The directors had lunch with the final list of applicants, and one man impressed everyone as outstanding. He was a management consultant whose style was to ask basic and challenging questions. The directors were certain that his approach to business would be immensely valuable.

Without involving any member of the department in the selection process, the management consultant was hired. Whispers of concern preceded him, and further investigations indicated some problems in his background. Nevertheless, the company prepared to welcome him.

It took nearly a year for the scale of the disaster to sink in. The ex-consultant was good at asking questions, but not at answering them. His colleagues and subordinates were driven wild by the pattern of provoking questions, delayed decisions, and frightened withdrawal in the face of 'attack'. His behaviour antagonized them to such an extent that confusion and frustration intensified within the development team.

Channels of decision making became choked with weed and blocked by the rotting hulks of unresolved issues. The senior scientist, a man whose main interests lay in obscure calculations, eventually found it necessary to write the following memorandum on 7 January: 'Could I please have a reply to my memo of 6 December, which asked for a reply to my memo of 11 October?'

The development manager responded to the attacks by withdrawing into increasingly detailed but meaningless work and finally left with a nervous breakdown. It took another six months to collect the pieces and to build the department again; a total of two years had been virtually wasted. Eventually, the company decided to write down the lessons which should, like the warnings given to Julius Caesar about the Ides of March, help to avoid making the same mistakes again.

- Beware of a silver tongue and check for real achievement
- Involve the team choosing its own leaders as far as possible
- Be careful about managers who appear distant, confusing, or arrogant
- Never underestimate the time and care needed to choose people wisely
- Remember that, as with milk, the 'cream should be at the top'. The quality of those who fill management positions is crucial.

A poor recruitment and selection decision often leads to a whole series of serious problems for years to come. Recruiting someone who lacks the capacity to do a job to the required standard means that the job is badly done, that overall standards deteriorate, that colleagues become frustrated, and that the person concerned usually becomes a permanent fixture because it is difficult for him or her to find another job. In addition, to rub salt into the wound, the person often feels undervalued and spends countless hours grumbling and complaining that no one understands him.

Work-study engineers have clicked their stop watches often enough to know that the best employee at any level will be many times more useful than the worst; therefore, it is vital to hire people who can 'deliver the goods'.

This discrepancy between the performance of the best and the worst is a serious problem in skilled and repetitive jobs, but it can be a first-order disaster at management level. An incompetent manager distresses staff, bungles many tasks and, tragically, runs lethargically away from opportunities. He or she not only makes a substandard contribution, but inhibits subordinates and colleagues to such an extent that the total negative effect is far greater than anyone would dare calculate.

People can and do develop, but they rarely undergo a personal revolution. It is naive to expect a major change in the character of mature people. Few believe that every street corner fiddler can become a Yehudi Menuhin, but some managers foolishly believe they can bring about change on a similar scale in their subordinates.

While some features of personality and skill can be changed by training and experience, it is always an arduous process, and any real development in personality is largely dependent on the perception and willingness of the individual concerned. If a person lacks basic intelligence, judgment, or sensitivity to other people, substantial change is unlikely. After all, there is not much point in exerting great effort to make square pegs fit round holes if round pegs can be acquired in the first place.

In an organization that has poor recruitment and selection practices, managers often complain that applicants' qualifications get lower and lower each year and that people take too long to reach an acceptable standard of work. Because of demographic changes there are fewer intelligent, able and adaptable people in the population. If your organization does not have the quality of people it needs, this is a warning signal telling you that your recruitment approach needs a careful review.

Of course, selection is a two-way process. Organizations need to attract superior talent and provide a 'package of advantages' which are virtually impossible for excellent people to turn down.

A package of advantages should include tangible rewards like pay and intangible factors like corporate climate and development opportunities.

All sorts of factors make up climate. Desks, notices, colours, heating, hours of work, supervisors, status of work, and hundreds of other large and small matters combine to produce a particular climate. But climates, like clothes, go out of fashion. People choose whom they wish to work for and can usually choose to go elsewhere. Consequently, it pays to keep in touch with their needs and with the environment at large.

A good index of your company's attitude toward people is to see how newcomers react after a few weeks. Many firms irritate, bore, and subtly humiliate people from their first moments as employees. Managers then blame their low staff morale on the fickle, irresponsible attitudes of people today. They need to realize that, as Cassius says in *Julius Caesar:* 'The fault, dear Brutus, is not in our stars, but in ourselves, that we are underlings'.

An organization's stock of talent is another important issue. To be capable of sustaining health and seizing new opportunities, a firm needs to have a stock of available talent. The firm that has large numbers of people who are only 'just good enough' for their present jobs finds real difficulty in achieving more and in growing bigger. People, particularly managers and supervisors, need to grow and develop with the organization. The lesson is obvious: recruitment and selection should have an eye on the future as well as on immediate needs.

But there is a point to be careful of here. Take care not to underutilize people. They will become frustrated and angry and then seek a new employer.

Common recruiting faults

Many errors can be made when recruiting people. A frequent blunder occurs because managers seldom keep detailed records of the reasons why people move in and out of the organization. Every firm we know that has taken the trouble to study carefully the motives of leavers has been able to improve its systems. Studies show that the cost of hiring one person is equivalent to several months' salary. If a manager overspent the same amount on computer paper, people would laugh about it for years, but no one gives more than a shrug when a recruit leaves before he has contributed anything.

A second error in recruiting is not defining what kind of person you want to hire. Generally, a person is recruited with a particular job in mind. But if no one develops a list of qualities and qualifications that the successful applicant will need, then some important points are bound to be missed at the interview stage.

Third, interviews are often superficial and unorganized. Sometimes, because of inexperience or incompetence, an interviewer is more nervous than the candidate himself and, to hide this, spends more time talking than the applicant.

Generations of managers have been encouraged to use some simple, systematic approach to recruitment and selection, yet we constantly see evidence that even the most rudimentary points are overlooked. One manager we know used to start his interviews by asking: 'Have you a criminal record?' After that, a free exchange of views was hard to achieve!

A fourth recruiting fault occurs when there is an unwillingness to use outside help or aids in the selection process. If you want to measure a young person's potential as an apprentice engineer, conversations alone are likely to be inferior to structured interviews combined with a good set of tests designed for that purpose. When recruiting for an important job or where large numbers of people with similar skills are recruited, a fairly small expenditure on external advice can repay its initial cost time and time again. Even if an individual stays with you for only a few years, he or she is going to represent a fair-sized investment.

Many companies try to solve their recruitment problems by enlarging their personnel department. Unfortunately, although fine in principle, some personnel departments are the homes of failed executives who are out of touch with the needs of line managers and who spend their time doing things that those managers could do better themselves. A good personnel department can add tremendous depth to management practice; however, an incompetent personnel function is worse than useless because it takes over important tasks and bungles them. The people who really care about recruitment are those who have to work directly with the new employees.

Perhaps the most common recruiting fault is to ignore the latest research. In recent years there has been valuable new thinking on recruitment and selection. Although the name of the most useful concept 'competence theory' sounds grand, the notion is simple. Competence theory says that we should recruit those people who demonstrate the characteristics of superior performers in comparable jobs. This requires four steps:

1. Identify superior and average performers in defined jobs in your organization.
2. Collect objective evidence which shows you how superior and average performers differ in personality, history, motivation, skills and knowledge.
3. Determine which of the superior characteristics can be developed by training.
4. Recruit only those people who possess the non-trainable attributes needed for success.

Competence theory concentrates on what people can do, not what they know. For example, even though a teacher may have a PhD in calculus this may not result in superior performance. Class discipline may be a much more significant competence than academic accomplishment in a limited area.

In our book *The Unblocked Manager* (Gower, 1982) we define these competences which are vital for superior managerial performance.

The most important lesson is that we cannot be satisfied with the fumbling, casual, subjective selection methods practised by so many in the past. With increasing use of automated equipment the work that we humans perform is increasingly complex. Problem solving has largely replaced mindless repetition. More able people are needed and they are getting more scarce. Those organizations with superior people have a distinct and sustainable competitive advantage.

Recruiting and selection procedures

Because selection and recruitment are difficult, costly, competitive, and very important, many companies have adopted more systematic procedures to prevent past mistakes. As you read the steps below, compare them with your own firm's approach. You can then formulate a working discipline from your own experiences and observations. There is no substitute for really getting to know the application. How can this be achieved? Recent reviews of different selection methods indicate biographical data (information about the individual's past history) gives consistently valid and predicative information. In general, people will behave in the future as they have done in the past. A formula should be sought to identify those characteristics which high performers demonstrate. This becomes the template for selection.

- Make a list of the tasks you expect the person to perform and describe the overall contribution expected. Check with those who are closely involved to see whether your expectations are accurate.
- List the experience and personal qualities that are required to do the job well.
- Consider the likely future of this person in five years and the implications of this for selection.
- Place realistic advertisements in the most relevant publications.
- See that the interviews are properly planned and are conducted by more than one person.
- Look for evidence of past performance.
- Consider the physical side of the interviews; for instance, candidates are more likely to talk freely if both interviewer and applicant are seated at the same table or if they face each other in comfortable chairs.
- Encourage the applicant to ask questions and be frank in your replies, giving a completely realistic picture of the available job.
- Use objective tests wherever possible.
- Involve those with whom the new person will have to work.
- Get advice and help on important choices from experienced advisers, but do not rely on their judgment excessively. You have to work with the person selected; the expert does not.
- Remember that selection is a two-way process. Really useful people are invariably in short supply, and they can pick employers who offer the best rewards.
- The recruitment process is not complete when the applicant

has accepted your offer. The first few weeks at work, in particular, are crucial, and there should be careful effort to involve the newcomer in the job and the organization.

In the ideal situation, all positions within the company should be filled by people with the necessary intelligence, ability, experience, education and personal qualities to do their jobs really well. In addition, sufficient potential should be developed to meet the possible future needs of the business. This is a very great task and will never be entirely achieved, but we can hope for a situation where most opportunities are profitably seized.

Recruitment is often an irregular and unpredictable task, with the element of intuition playing a part in the end. But with care, recruitment disasters can be avoided. The effect of recruiting a really good person is often much greater than expected. Good people are real resources – true sources of strength – for any organization.

Key concepts

- Effective recruitment is vital for organizational success.
- Superior performers are usually many times more effective than the average.
- People's capacity to change their basic motivation and personality is limited.
- Recruitment is a two-way process.
- The effective organization attracts superior people through reward and corporate climate.
- Past performance is a good guide to future performance.
- Competence theory can make a significant contribution.
- Recruitment policy should relate to strategic planning.
- Lack of objective analysis is the most common fault in recruitment.
- Those who care most about new employees are the team with whom he or she will work.
- There is a 'technology' of good recruitment practice. This should be understood by all who take selection decisions.

Blockage 8 - Unfair rewards

'Companies that pay peanuts
get monkeys.'
Anon.

Organizations need people, and people need organizations. By and large, the best people tend to go to the organizations offering the best rewards. Conversely, organizations that pay below par tend to recruit inadequate employees.

Money is an emotional subject because a person's financial position in society is an important benchmark of success. While we can avoid being judged on some aspects of our lives, our status at work is not one of them. We are constantly being assessed, graded, and categorized, and the position we hold is one of the main criteria by which others judge us. Like it or not, employers make a tangible decision about our worth, from which spring many consequences affecting and influencing our whole lifestyle - the kind of house we live in, the type of car we drive, and even the educational opportunities for our children. We judge ourselves by our salaries and status level and often measure success by the speed at which we climb towards the apex of the pyramid. For many people a desire to get nearer the top is one of the main driving forces that give direction, challenge and energy to their working lives.

Rewards, like coins, have two sides, and on the obverse is the less pleasant reality of punishments. In a way, the absence of rewards is perhaps the main punishment that organizations can apply. Behaviour that is valued is rewarded with higher material rewards and increased prestige; behaviour that is not valued leaves people relatively deprived of these things. Achieving equity in this balancing act is often very difficult.

Many organizations have a complex web of negotiating procedures, committees, appraisal schemes, agreements, and the like for dealing with inevitably complex decisions concerning:

- *Wage differentials.* Should Harry earn more than Tom, and, if so, how much more?
- *Status.* Who should be paid by the hour, and who should have 'staff' status?
- *Motivation.* Are we paying enough for people to commit their energy?
- *Social responsibility.* What do we do about old Joe now that he is disabled?
- *The disadvantaged.* Should we give more help to minority or other less-powerful groups?
- *Division of labour.* Does our payment system prevent work from being organized in the optimum way?
- *Rigidity.* Are we sufficiently open to new ideas and concepts about rewards? Are we moving with the times?
- *Trade unions.* Should we encourage or discourage trade unions? What should our negotiating tactics be?

Monetary rewards are subject to the prevailing management philosophy of the time. In the early 1950s the 'factor-based' merit rating method became widely practised. On average ratings were taken against ten factors which were often personality based, and employees were divided into five categories: from excellent to poor. Factors such as initiative, dependability, commitment and co-operation were widely assessed.

The factor rating system lasted until the 1980s when we saw an evolution in merit rating systems based on systematic assessment of performance against predetermined objectives and a vast expansion in the practice of appraisal, even down to operator level. At the same time many organizations abandoned across-the-board annual pay increases and substituted payment for individual performance. Reward moved from merit to performance. 'Performance management' was the dominant managerial philosophy. Wherever possible, subjectivity was rationalized, and all salary progress made dependent on performance against objectives. Objectives are best divided into three categories:

* ongoing objectives - permanent standards which must be maintained
* short-term targets or goals - related to specific assignments
* self-development goals - acquiring new competences.

Each objective needs to be clarified, monitored, appraised and related to both psychological and material rewards. This can be quite elaborate. One large employer we know has a six-page appraisal form, with 4-8 ongoing objectives (each with 3-4 performance indicators) and detailed objectives. This provides a rational basis for a comprehensive and factual assessment of actual contribution.

Reward systems based on performance have rarely appealed to trade unions or those whose political philosophy emphasizes parity of income above all. Accepting the principle that a relatively new employee may be five times more productive than a 30-year veteran runs contrary to traditional trade union values in most Western cultures. Managers have no choice but to fight such unproductive stances. It is managements' task to be compassionate, and be seen to be compassionate, but never to accept the principle that a person should be rewarded according to their need. Employees at all levels must accept that there is a direct connection between contribution and reward.

Fortunately the majority of employees are willing to accept the payment for merit principle when it is fairly applied. This has been demonstrated by the success of Japanese work practices in their new plants established in Europe and North America. Initially the almost transparent honesty and enthusiasm of the Japanese provoked derision. They were laughed at for their single-status canteens, compulsory uniforms for all staff and ruthless destruction of symbols of status differences. However, the mirth and cynicism of observers turned to admiration as Japanese companies began to prove themselves distinctly superior. When asked for the secret of their success the Japanese industrialists emphasized the creation of a 'family atmosphere' in which every employee felt valued and recognized. To the chagrin of many Westerners, it was the Japanese who provided an object lesson in equity.

'Fair' rewards can never be determined with total objectivity. Of course, employees will compare themselves with others in the hierarchy and assiduously check the going rate for similar jobs in other organizations. It is desirable to have a logical, defendable and accepted framework for job grading in all but the smallest concerns. Deep damage to the organization's climate follows whenever a reward system is perceived (rightly or wrongly) to be unfair.

If rewards are felt to be unfair, there is a likelihood of a deeper malaise – lack of trust. Employees only trust management when they feel that those with power are consistent, compassionate and reliable. Where employees suspect that they are ruled by incompetent or heartless managers dissatisfaction will seek an outlet which is often continuous carping about the reward system, and a general lack of motivation. Human energy is never absent, but it can be channelled into negative or positive expression. Top managers are responsible for directing the energy of the organization towards positive goals.

Reward systems are always based on principles whether they are implicit or explicit. People tend to do what they are rewarded for. Hence the design of the reward system defines, over time, the organization's development of capability. This has deep strategic significance.

The reward system should encourage those competences needed for excellence today and tomorrow. Top managers require a vision of the future that is sufficiently well articulated to provide a detailed specification of the necessary human resource capability in terms of human resources. Frequently this is absent in organizations. Progressive managers often realize the importance of a vision of the future but have not realized the importance of expressing this in behavioural (i.e. specific) terms.

An example of excellent practice makes the point. In the early 1980s British Airways realized that superior customer service was a potential competitive advantage. The company had the opposite reputation amongst many airline passengers. When travelling overseas at that time we regularly asked travel agents to book us with 'any carrier other than BA'. If British Airways had left their vision at the level of a generalized intention nothing would have changed.

British Airways executives analysed exactly what passengers wanted from an airline and set out to inculcate the sensitivity, responsiveness, attitudes and skills needed to reshape the airline into one that could reliably deliver superior customer service. An essential ingredient in BA's organization development programme was the realignment of the reward system to encourage this process. People needed to be measured on what they should do - not their present role. This meant that all personnel systems were managed as a whole, making a defined contribution to a strategic vision. Today BA claim to be 'The World's Favourite Airline' and in our experience they are probably right!

Rewards are hardly ever exclusively concerned with financial benefit. Receiving a salary motivates an individual to attend work and do the minimum necessary to sustain an acceptable income. Superior motivation is encouraged by a reward system that hooks the individual and provides real job satisfaction. Not only the content of a job (what the person is required to do) but also the level of work group pride in high performance deeply influence daily behaviour. Hence managers are wise when they define such intangible rewards as powerful tools for influence. Managers at every level must improve their skills as job enrichers and providers of meaning.

Reward systems influence the ways in which people think. Unless an aspect of behaviour is rewarded it tends to diminish in importance and become an indistinguishable background feature. Rewards are an intervention in the perceptual programming of people: hence they are the fundamental method of achieving compliance within organizations.

Some trade unions, amongst others, have recognized this, and sought to undermine the managerial power base by gaining control of the principles which underlie reward systems. From the management viewpoint this is destructive, as management control over priorities and standards is essential in gearing the capability of human resources to meet strategic aims. Unfortunately as trade unions are not responsible for organizational efficiency they often tend to ignore this vital element in their campaigning. Managers are wise to ensure that they understand, in depth, the individual motivating factors which influence their staff. These may be affected by cultural, social, political, economic, educational or age-related criteria.

Organizations must recognize that:

1. Rewards are best related to individual performance and not given as general pay increases.
2. Employees should be told the principles on which rewards are allocated and that high performance will bring higher rewards. (Here effective communication is clearly important.)
3. Training should provide a means by which high motivation can be transformed into high performance and high reward.
4. It is important that managers clearly identify goals for each individual and remove both personal and organizational blockages to goal attainment.
5. Managers should seek to demonstrate that support for non-productive views does not lead to success in the longer term.

Despite all their good intentions managers often find that the principle of fair rewards is very difficult to implement in practice. Large organizations may find that the value of someone's contribution cannot be measured directly. Ask yourself how you evaluate the benefit that ICI derives from an efficient telephone operator or the value that a community gains from an assiduous policeman. It is impossible to be totally fair. Sometimes contribution can only be assessed indirectly and by whether the reward system is felt to be fair by the majority.

Even when criteria for job performance are explicit the search for fairness is further complicated by another factor. It is fallacious to expect people always to behave rationally. Complaints about rewards may be displaced anger from quite another source. Motivations are so obscure that even experienced psychologists find them difficult to explain. So, how do managers proceed? We believe that they should concentrate on six 'reward strategies'. When combined and implemented these provide an adequate 'rule of thumb' theory to justify fairness on most occasions.

1. Be explicit about what constitutes success in each job.
2. Reward 'positive' behaviour by above average material benefits.
3. Reward 'positive' behaviour by above average recognition.
4. Avoid exploiting a category of people because they are weak.
5. Create opportunities for people to feel good about using their profession, trade and skills.

6. Communicate the principles of your reward system widely. A fair reward system is one which is:

- based on a fair and equitable method of measuring performance
- as consistent as possible
- easy to understand
- straightforward to monitor
- flexible, good performers feeling that they have been rewarded
- based on a firm and accepted payment system
- supported by a staff and management development policy.

When there is an inadequate framework for dealing with these kinds of issues managers frequently find themselves confused, depressed, and even mildly hysterical about the reward system. They feel defensive and threatened, especially when workers are organized and potentially strong. As a result, decisions are made in response to threats, a course which inevitably breeds more inequity and more militancy.

Like it or not, we will never have the perfect 'meritocracy'. However, we still need to make decisions about the relative worth of our people.

Although there are many forces at work and no right answers, a clear policy should emerge and be tested in the day-to-day skirmishes of the factory, office or laboratory. The organizations which are in the worst shape are those which do not confront rewards issues and, instead, let other forces make their decisions for them.

Symptoms of inadequate rewards

If you recognize the following symptoms, rewards could be an issue in your organization:

- The wage system prevents work from being organized in an optimum way
- Large numbers of people feel undervalued
- Decisions about pay are forced on you
- You get people with inadequate skills

- There is an absence of machinery for dealing with issues about rewards
- The reward system inhibits constructive change
- You are not seen as a 'good employer' in the locality.

Fortunately, money is not the only way in which people measure their value. Sufficient cash will not in itself achieve the high level of motivation needed by every dynamic and successful organization, but it will prevent a person from feeling grossly undervalued.

Key concepts

- Financial rewards are the symbol of success in many societies
- Reward systems concern more than material benefit: psychological rewards are equally important
- New styles of reward system emphasize performance rather than responsibility, outputs rather than inputs
- Careful attention to job effectiveness criteria is the basis of a well-designed reward system
- A healthy corporate culture can be demonstrated by equal treatment in areas where performance is not the key
- Complaints about rewards are frequently a symbol of lack of trust between management and other levels of employees
- Wise managers explore and explain the principles on which the reward system is based
- Reward systems are an element of the organization's strategy. People should be rewarded for helping to achieve overall strategic goals
- A high level of job challenge is a reward in itself
- Rewards condition the thought processes of individuals
- Trade unions often seek to undermine the principle of 'reward for performance'
- Fair rewards require explicit job criteria, selective systems, psychological rewards, pride in success, and an effective communication system
- Reward systems should be consistent, easy to comprehend, straightforward, flexible, system-wide and supported by training

- If a reward system is inadequate it will create a strategic weakness throughout the organization.

Blockage 9 – Poor training

'All living organisms adapt,
or they cease to exist.'
Louis E. Davis

A colleague of ours has spent a lot of time visiting firms in the meat industry, offering advice on how to teach manual skills in a better way. He often tells the story of a master butcher who demonstrated how he taught knife sharpening.

Although the butcher was obviously very skilled, it was noticeable that he had quite a collection of scars on his hand where the knife had slipped. When asked how he accounted for them, the butcher replied: 'Well, you have to learn in any job, don't you? Getting cut is part of it'.

The master butcher found it hard to imagine that there were better ways of learning than the trial-and-error methods of his apprenticeship. Fortunately, he decided to try some of the 'systematic' training techniques advocated by specialists. Much to his surprise, he found that careful instruction reduced learning time and that there was no need to acquire a patchwork of scars when learning to use a knife.

A great deal of learning takes place each day in organizations. People acquire new skills, gain insights into new ideas and knowledge, and learn how to achieve better results. In many cases, formal approaches to learning can often be more helpful than the traditional trial-and-error methods.

This is particularly true when a new person joins an organization. Inevitably, he or she lacks some knowledge and skills and needs to know what company procedures are, what is required and even where to hang a coat. A choice has to be made

– will the new recruit learn from a thoughtfully constructed induction programme, or pick up a skill from Nellie, the old hand? New knowledge and skills are often difficult to acquire. Whenever a job takes a fair amount of time to learn or when specific skills have to be acquired, it is worth developing a systematic approach to help the new person reach a satisfactory standard with a minimum of time, cost and stress.

Training has become much more professional in the past decade. No longer are courses seen as holidays from real work where participants engage in the seductive diversions of a country house lifestyle whilst, incidentally, sitting through a few boring lectures. Increasingly, a competent workforce is viewed as a source of sustainable competitive advantage. The skills, knowledge, competences and attitudes of employees are recognized as logical components of organizational strategy. And quite right too! Training must be viewed as an investment rather than a cost.

A great change in training technique has been provoked by a widespread realization that people learn best by first-hand experience. This approach, called 'experiential' by its practitioners, has revolutionized the management of learning. The trainee ceases to be a passive recipient of ideas, soaking up the principles of good practice like blotting paper. In an experiential-based training programme the emphasis is on action, experiment and review. Trainees are invited to come to terms with ideas for themselves and have new experiences which cause them to question their current stances and habits.

There has been a second revolution in training practice. We no longer think about skills and knowledge as the end result of training. Rather the emphasis is on competence – what an individual is able and willing to do. So, a training programme for sales professionals begins with an analytical stage to answer the questions 'What differentiates an excellent sales professional from someone who is merely average?' The resulting list of competences might include:

- ability to establish mutual trust with potential customers
- capacity to clearly describe the benefits of the product
- ability to respond to the specific needs of the potential customer
- ability to close a sale.

Each competence must be identified and divided into recruitment or training issues. Then training is focused on developing competences proven to lead to superior performance.

The third revolution in training techniques has been a recognition that much learning needs to be energized by the person themselves. It is not good enough to wait passively to be spoonfed with training. Individuals must be assertive and proactive in managing their own development. Fortunately, personal growth is a rewarding process. People must realize that they are masters of their own development. The organization plays a vital role but it is individual will which makes the most significant difference. So the trend towards company resource centres and self-directed learning is a healthy one which has proved valuable for all groups from machine operators to senior managers.

The management of training is undergoing substantial change. Not long ago a training manager was likely to be a failed line manager whose only saving graces were an affable personality and a fund of jokes. Now training managers are likely to be developed professionals who have acquired competences in:

- identifying superior performers
- identifying necessary behavioural attributes
- devising multifaceted development programmes
- relating training investment to strategic aims
- encouraging self-directed development
- using training to 'unblock' the organization.

Most governments have woken up to the need to develop a range of competences in the national workforce. There have been considerable developments in the education systems of advanced countries aimed at providing the capabilities required for tomorrow and the readiness to accept ongoing change. This is relevant to organizations for two reasons. Firstly, it is wise to forge a partnership between the organization and educational bodies and, secondly, there is often money available from public funds to support training. Sensible organizations do not look gift horses in the mouth!

Training policy has to be determined at the very top of the organization. Unfortunately, few organizations undertake comparative studies of how their training investment compares with their competitors. This is a source of competitive weakness. Investment in training is substantial and the strategic consequences of poor training are severe. All training initiatives should include an evaluation process which seeks to justify the expenditure and give feedback to those who provide the training.

Costs of poor training

Although we often measure the cost of machine maintenance and depreciation down to the second decimal place, training is sometimes viewed as an unfortunate operating cost rather than as an investment in the future. It is relatively easy to buy a new machine or even to build a new factory, but it is often more difficult to obtain the creative element of a business – the people who make an organization thrive or fall.

Lack of training can prevent technological innovation. General Motors established a partly robotized production line in its Lordstown, Ohio, plant in 1972. But the line ran into so many difficulties that it was put into hibernation for seven years. Why? The executive director for advanced manufacturing, Gerry Elson, explained that GM had greatly underestimated the need for shopfloor re-education. One employee said: 'In order to operate a new technology you have to think that technology. A superficial understanding is just not enough. It has to structure the way you perceive things'.

Management training and competence

Every individual must take a measure of responsibility for personal learning and development. At the management level, learning is almost the cornerstone of success. Today, in such rapidly changing times, there is no room for fixed attitudes and yesterday's approaches. In a hurricane, the trees that bend and move end up standing, while those that are rigid and unyielding are left broken and uprooted.

Theories on the nature of managerial competence abound with lists describing the qualities, traits and abilities of successful managers. The four principal abilities that these lists often contain are control; innovation; harnessing people's energies and putting them to use; and integration with the organization as a whole. If control is lacking, there is confusion; if there is no innovation, rigor mortis quickly sets in; if people's energies are not harnessed, the result is often sloth and rebellion; and if integration is not present, there is empire building.

However, even though these ideas contain a basis of truth, a man or a woman can have all the necessary qualities and still not be a good manager. Something else is needed to make the difference between success and failure.

Management competence involves not only having the necessary knowledge and skill, but also having the vital capacity to seize opportunities, to stimulate action, to venture ahead, to make decisions, to stand up and be counted, and to take a measure of risk. Without such action, management just does not exist; it is only theory. No textbook or paper qualification can give a person that capacity; in the end, it involves learning by experience, exposing oneself to difficulty and risk, and learning from successes and mistakes. The organization can aid the learning process by providing the opportunity and a measure of support; but when the chips are down, the manager is responsible for his own development.

Systematic training

Organizing the learning process is more difficult than it appears at first sight. The most difficult aspect is recognizing that something needs to be done and identifying what it is. To help bring some clarity, many companies have organized their training on a 'systematic' footing which involves:

1. An assessment of the overall training needs based on the future strategic plans and current blockages of the organization.
2. An allocation of corporate responsibility for training and for the detailed mechanics of implementing it.
3. The preparation of training plans on an individual and group basis.
4. Use of many kinds of media and training techniques.
5. Training conducted by skilled trainers according to the plan.
6. Keeping training records.

7.   Reviews of the results and costs of the effort.

Shortcomings of systematic training

Systematic training is fine in many situations and has brought many benefits to organizations, but there are also dangers to avoid. First, training can become a religion, with everyone preaching its virtues and no one questioning them. Small firms, particularly, are often not formal in most of the things they do. This can result in their being more dynamic and creative. Having highly systematic training when other business functions are not systematic is like having a standard-sized human body with one arm five feet long - it is out of proportion with everything else.

A second systematic training snag concerns the false sense of security that systems often bring: 'Of course we do this or that - we have a system for it.' But every so often the system does not bring results, not because it's bad, but because other, more important matters - like the commitment of managers to the system, or the quality or relationships between people - are neglected. The system can easily take control if you stop questioning the relevance of what you originally intended it to accomplish.

As Ron Johnson, a friend of ours, says: 'Training is no longer a question of injecting people with doses of skill and knowledge. It is the management of learning, helping people cope with changes in their working lives.'

Key concepts

• Systematic training is essential in today's organizations
• Training must begin as soon as a person joins a new organization
• A competent workforce is a source of sustainable competitive advantage
• On average training represents 3-4 per cent of the total wage bill - a large investment!
• Learning by experience is a powerful principle on which to base training events
• Training should provide the competences proven to lead to superior performance

- Training cannot be managed by organizations alone – self-responsibility is essential
- Training managers are becoming more professional
- There should be a close partnership between organizations and educational establishments
- Training policy must be determined at the top of organizations
- Ongoing evaluation is necessary to ensure efficiency of training
- Inadequacies in training cost organizations dearly
- Management training is an important part of organizational strategy.
- Systematic training should be part of a comprehensive human resource management policy.

Blockage 10 – Lack of personal development

'Every man should ask himself each day whether he is not too readily accepting negative solutions.'
Winston Churchill

Organizations exist to achieve. They pool the skills and knowledge of individuals and create an environment that can bring about success and achievement. Sometimes organizations help people to develop, grow stronger, and become more capable, but the opposite also happens. Organizations inhibit individual development which causes people to stagnate instead of grow.

When directed towards organizational goals, individual strength and capability provide a resource of tremendous value: the creative vitality to resolve problems and to continually adapt and improve.

Many people are accustomed to thinking about individual capability in terms of skills and knowledge. Training and development strategies are often geared simply to increasing skill and knowledge. However, if you listen to the gossip in the byways, and if you observe people in action, it becomes apparent that the attitudes of individuals are just as important, if not more important, than skill and knowledge.

A deeper examination reveals that business life is full of examples of executives who seem to have all the right skills and all the knowledge, technical and otherwise, and yet they still never seem to achieve worthwhile results. On the other hand, many executives, particularly owner-managers, have had little formal training and appear deficient in the accepted managerial skills, yet they have created immensely successful businesses and always seem to have the knack of succeeding. In practice, management is not simply a question of skills and textbook knowledge, it also involves perceiving opportunities, seizing them, and achieving goals. Each organization needs dynamic people in key jobs. Not everyone can or will develop, but every organization should have a proportion of achievers.

Differences between high and low achievers

From observing successful people in organizations, we can compile a list of those characteristics that always seem to be present. Individuals are sources of energy, and human energy can be channelled in different ways. If it is blocked it remains unexpressed and results in frustration. Energy can be frittered away, resulting in no gain to the individual or to others. Conversely, energy can be directed towards achieving satisfaction and tangible results.

High achievers are people who have found positive and satisfying uses for their energy, whereas low achievers are those who spend their energy unproductively. Looking at the way in which human energy is used can provide a clear insight into achievement. Our capability is greatly affected by the psychological attitude or stance that we habitually adopt while confronting life. As you read the next few paragraphs, think of a few of your acquaintances and consider how they use their energy.

Low achievers

People who can be categorized as low achievers seem to exhibit a passive stance toward life, either seeking to be undisturbed or frittering away their energy on unproductive pursuits. They will generally avoid feedback from others and criticism is viewed as negative, rather than helpful and useful. Apparently distant from their own feelings, these individuals do not know themselves and do not seek to do anything about it. New experiences are avoided because of the potential threat they can bring. They have little concern for the development of others and seldom help others to become more effective. Often they relate to others through manipulative games and keep at a distance because they fear the consequences of being known by others.

Although less effective people are often good at giving sympathy to others, they rarely offer any real help. Their beliefs are basically the beliefs of others, often learned in childhood, and seldom seriously questioned. They are not authentic people. Often they are intolerant of the views of others and are heard to bemoan the fact that others are not like them. They are content with low standards for themselves and for others and when the going gets tough they are the first to opt out.

Low achievers see themselves as victims of misfortune. They view people who are stronger and more effective than themselves as contributing substantially to their basically unhappy and unsatisfactory working lives. Above all, the less effective are characterized by a low degree of insight into themselves and their beliefs and by an unwillingness to do anything about increasing their own effectiveness.

High achievers

Successful people, by contrast, seem to take an active stance toward life. They are the people who make things happen and are constantly seeking new challenges for themselves and the groups that they represent. Because they want to know more about themselves, they are interested in the feedback that others can give them about both their strengths and their weaknesses. They welcome constructive criticism and use it to improve their own performance.

Recognizing that time and energy are limited in terms of human existence, high achievers plan their lives to make the most of these valuable resources. They seek new experiences because they see the quality of life being linked to the range of experience that an individual can encompass. By constantly achieving good results, they build a reputation as people who can be relied on and who are committed to seeing things through even when the going gets tough. They seek understanding of their own feelings and emotions and try to use them as a positive force in their relationships with others.

Although they try to give attention to others, effective people are not trapped into superficial relationships out of desire to please and be popular. They utilize the views of others as an aid towards clarification and creativity. They strive towards more direct and open relationships, realizing that little is gained in the long term from secrecy and holding back.

High achieving people frequently value the importance of allowing and aiding personal growth in others. Consequently, when managing they are prepared to give freedom to others, recognizing that personal growth requires not only room to grow, but also the facility to 'fly kites' and experiment.

Standards are important to effective people. Although standards are set realistically, they also stretch the person sufficiently to represent a real challenge. These standards are often apparent to others who identify with and seek to emulate them. Successful people have worked through their goals and values and avoid being sidetracked or inhibited by deviations from others. They know themselves, are clear about their beliefs, and are confident about themselves and their contribution. In everyday language, they are called strong people and they enjoy that feeling of strength, using their personal energy as a positive force. Not overwound and tense, these people view life as an adventure and are prepared to experience the depth of whatever opportunity presents itself.

Comparison of stance

Comparing the psychological stance of more and less successful people helps clarify the main differences in their approach, but the real test is in results. Successful people achieve their goals and fulfil much of their potential. Unsuccessful people do not realize their potential and they fail.

Of course, no one displays either one or the other set of characterstics totally, but personal development can essentially be seen as a movement away from the negative characteristics towards the positive.

When placed side by side, the two sets of characteristics become stark alternatives; choices that individuals make about themselves, their approach to life, and their approach to work. Those individuals who predominantly exhibit the high effectiveness characteristics may be uncomfortable people to work with. At first sight, their drive and dynamism appear to inhibit the common good of the whole. Some organizations, particularly those in which tangible results are less important, discourage high effectiveness characteristics. But the effective organizations create a climate in which individuals are encouraged to move towards high effectiveness characteristics and personal stagnation seldom occurs.

High effectiveness characteristics	Personal stagnation characteristics
1 Are active	1 Are passive
2 Seek challenge	2 Avoid challenge
3 See and use time and energy as valuable resources	3 Misuse time and energy
4 Are in touch with their feelings	4 Are out of touch with their feelings
5 Show concern for others	5 Do not care for others' feelings
6 Are relaxed	6 Are tense
7 Are open and honest	7 Use manipulation
8 'Stretch' themselves	8 Avoid 'stretching' themselves
9 Have clear personal values	9 Are programmed by the views of others
10 Set high standards	10 Set low standards
11 Welcome feedback	11 Avoid feedback
12 See things through	12 Opt out
13 Tolerate and use opposing views	13 Are intolerant to others' views
14 Use conflict constructively	14 Avoid conflict
15 Give freedom	15 Restrain freedom
16 Are happy about life	16 Are unhappy about life
17 Seek insight into themselves	17 Avoid insight into themselves

Personal growth is a complex and difficult process to describe, but implies the following:

- The individual takes initiatives
- Personal blocks and difficulties are resolved and cleared

- There is a deliberate attempt to learn from experience despite the discomfort that this sometimes brings.

Growth is a constant process that can continue throughout career and life. New challenges and difficulties occur for all of us and they need to be worked through if we are to continue to grow. We have a choice: whether to learn and develop from our experience of life or to allow ourselves to be defeated. It is sometimes hard to experience this choice as real, especially when we see ourselves trapped by circumstances, but personal effectiveness demands that we become more informed about and in charge of our own lives.

We believe that all personal development is firmly based on one idea: every person has unrealized potential. Of course, limitations on an individual's capacity do exist: age, size, health, family situation, education and the external environment can present real constraints. However, if you probe your apparent limitations, many of those that seemed absolute turn out to be amenable to change. Many personal limitations may be removed when they are tested, if only people take the trouble to try.

Common blockages to realizing potential

Some of the more common factors that block the capacity of people to realize their individual potential are as follows.

Family influence

In early life, children acquire an understanding of the world around them. Through experience, the young child learns about possibilities and develops an appropriate way of behaving. Although a child tends to imitate the behaviour and attitudes of parents and significant others, there are times when the child reacts against them. Almost always the child involuntarily adopts a view of himself that is limiting and one-sided. These formative attitudes are so fundamental that their effects are rarely questioned and a person can go through adult life playing out a 'programme' established in childhood.

Personal inertia

Sometimes people are resigned to the impossibility of change and development. Perhaps they try but fail. Dispirited by failure, they ask 'what is the point?' This attitude can strongly inhibit change because they capitulate before making a full commitment and so undermine their chances of success. All change requires inertia to be overcome and this takes energy and persistence.

Collapse of energy

A person often begins a process of personal development but then becomes demoralized with failure. Any obstacle causes the person's drive and energy to collapse and little of worth is achieved. When the attitude of 'Nothing works out anyway' is adopted, it helps to ensure that the same collapse will occur again. In reality, obstacles can be serious and a person can be overwhelmed through trying to face them. However, if the feeling of disappointment is challenged, it becomes possible to 'bounce back' with renewed effort.

Lack of support

Personal development often involves building closer links with others. When a person is attempting to change, there is a risk of confusion, discomfort and uncertainty. Supportive relationships with others provide encouragement through the inevitable difficulties of change. Comparison with others helps individuals to understand their own unique contributions.

Inadequate feedback

Everyone makes judgements and observations about other people. Sometimes these evaluations are complimentary but frequently they are critical. An observer can see how others react, make choices and deal with problems. However, rarely does one feel free to fully express these feelings and perceptions to others and, in many circles, it is considered impolite to do so. It is unfortunate that the information is withheld because it could be used to further an individual's personal development. Experience suggests that people need substantial amounts of straight feedback to provide them with sufficient data for their own development.

Hostility from others

Each individual is involved in a complex web of social relationships with people who have an investment in that person not changing; they need that individual to continue being the person they know. Any change in yourself can threaten or discomfort those who relate to you. Often, without realizing what is happening, other people will seek to sabotage your efforts to change by ridiculing, devaluing or even by direct conflict.

Insufficient resources

In reality, it is easier for some people to make changes than others. For exmaple, the range of choices available to a bright twenty-year-old is many times greater than that available to a sixty-year-old person in poor health. Occasionally a person makes a significant breakthrough in spite of the severe limitations of a situation. However, this is exceptional and it is wiser for individuals to review realistically the options and resources available to them. Exciting fantasies are enticing, but real growth is rooted in practical daily happenings and experiences.

Self-development is a person's best way to acquire the competences with which to attack an unfriendly system. No one can depend on employers to provide all necessary growth experiences. Self-motivated people must undertake personal development with or without formal support. This may seem anarchic or revolutionary, but it's not so; organizations and individuals benefit in the end. People must realize that organizations cannot exploit everyone's potential. If the inherent abilities of individuals were fully harnessed, the organization would be swamped with talent and could not cope. In practice, organizations hardly ever have adequate systems for people development. Competition is the rule, and this is probably best for all concerned. It is questionable whether a totally structured personal development system is desirable, since it would preclude self-responsibility. While organizations usually provide opportunities for development, it is up to the individuals to capture them. People who sensibly nourish their personal growth are far more likely to survive and succeed.

This can be done by taking the following steps:

- identify your next career step specifically
- list people who hold the wanted role at the moment
- categorize them into 'unsuccessful' and 'successful' performers (be as objective as possible (– you don't have to tell them!)
- get to know both unsuccessful and successful performers personally
- find out exactly what both low and high performers do
- ask what sort of behaviour contributed to success
- carefully list the behaviour traits in writing – do not jump to conclusions
- compare 'best' with 'worst' – what are the differences?
- go outside your own organization and look at successful performers in the wanted role to validate your conclusions
- check textbooks, autobiographies and so on to give different perspectives
- write a detailed description of these competences in the wanted role which result in high performance
- compare this with your current capabilities and prepare an action plan to fill gaps.

Organizations should encourage the personal development of their principal employees. Boredom, distinterest and narrow-mindedness are the products of a repressive regime. Unblocked organizations need sufficient numbers of unblocked people!

Key concepts

- Successful organizations enable individuals to develop their potential
- Real development is often self-motivated; but the organization can create the conditions for individuals to fulfil their potential
- High achievers are active, seeking challenge and personal excellence

- Low achievers are passive, demoralized and fail to seek personal excellence
- Blockages to personal development may include family influences, personal inertia, collapse of energy, lack of support, inadequate feedback, hostility from others, or insufficient resources
- The active person cannot depend on someone else to facilitate self-development; the responsibility can never be delegated or abandoned
- Individuals have to seek to acquire the real competences associated with success.

Blockage 11 – Inadequate communication

> 'There are those who listen
> and those who wait to talk.'
> John Donne

There is an organization in New Zealand with an interesting problem. For years there had been little progress. A once great company had declined. The unadventurous and authoritarian management cut costs, refused to invest in the future and the workforce became increasingly disenchanted. Then a new management came along, reviewed company strategy and decided on necessary changes. These were announced to all the employees by a somewhat introverted chief executive. He expected a rapturous reception but was greeted with disbelief and cynicism.

What was the basis of the problem? The new strategy was well founded. Benefits would flow to all. The company would grow again. However, none of these 'truths' was accepted by the workforce. They remembered only the broken promises and penny-pinching attitudes of the previous management. At this point the organization was suffering from inadequate communication.

Organizations must take communication seriously for four principal reasons.

Vision

Simply being aware of the environment is necessary, but not

sufficient. Changes in politics, social forces, technology, market, lifestyle and competition are frequently fundamental and should guide the organization's vision.

Senior management must devise and define the identity of the organization, and state where it is heading. This is a 'vision of the future' that is important, coherent and sustainable. It is the task of senior management to give meaning to the organization's activities. Those at the top must have a message to communicate. Inspiration, excitement, farsightedness, great clarity, and good judgement are necessary ingredients of an inspiring 'vision of the future'. When this does not exist people are inadequately led, aimless and demotivated. The 'vision' is the primary energizing force in the organization. It may be expressed in words but, most importantly, the vision should be shared by all those who hold positions of power.

At the top there must be a forum for debate so that the vision of the organization is defined and shared. Unless deep communication exists at this level there is a fundamental flaw in the management system. Of course, the possession of a vision – no matter how sound or wise – is never enough. The vision must be communicated.

Managers must develop the communication techniques and skills to encourage people to play a part in transforming the 'vision' into reality. Senior managers should develop skills of persuasion in order to shape attitudes, change behaviour, instil standards and build a positive climate. Managers must be able to 'sell' the importance of working together for the common cause.

Techniques for persuasion are part of true leadership skills and yet we rarely teach managers how to influence others. However, persuasion techniques are empty unless they are supported by behaviour. Stories, myths and legends are more persuasive than words, and persuasive managers use these devices to shape attitudes.

Working together

All organizations depend for their efficiency on developing individuals who are grouped together as departments or functions. But customers want the output of the whole organization: not one specialist group. So organizations must integrate the work of different departments, and the means of achieving this integration is communication.

The needs for integration vary with the size of the organization and the type of work undertaken. Small organizations can be controlled by a single boss, whereas large ones require much more elaborate systems for integration. Routine, professional, divisionalized and creative organizations all have different needs. Mechanisms for integration range from direct supervision to matrix management. Organizations which lack well-developed integrating mechanisms are inefficient, wasteful and incompetent.

Communication across organizations is affected by the physical layout of offices and work places. Naturally those who work together communicate more easily, and difficult geographical factors make communication complex, uncertain and expensive.

Unfortunately in recent years many architects and planners have paid scant attention to the human consequences of their designs, resulting in breakdowns of both formal and informal communication. The effects of geography on communication can extend throughout the organization. Individual workers should be helped to communicate by the layout of their work place. Teams that need to relate should be physically close. At the organizational level, divisional and internal communication problems can be mitigated by careful consideration at the building design stage. Intelligent use of electronic media can reduce communication blockages.

Whilst geography can cause significant communication problems even in the most conveniently laid out organization, there are frequently 'islands of ignorance'. The solution is effective downward flow of information. Objectives, policies, procedures, disciplines, success measures, controls and directives all have to be reliably cascaded down. This is an essential integrating force which binds all parts of the organization together.

Downward communication enables organizations to be controlled by forward planning, performance evaluation and the enforcement of policies. There are four main methods: down the line, through representatives of the workforce, through mass communication or through using training techniques.

One of the most useful methods of downward communication

is 'briefing groups'. Messages are transmitted down the organization layer by layer in a structured and timed sequence. Of course, the messages must be valid and truthful. Regular briefings ensure that everyone has a face-to-face meeting with their direct manager and receives up-to-date information about the organization's fortunes.

Fairness, community and commitment

Organizations are communities which have institutions of government, legal systems, welfare policies and hierarchies of power. A community can be either enjoyed or disliked by its members. Astute managers work hard to build a healthy community. This nourishes individuals and creates a climate of high motivation. Perhaps the most important factor is trust.

Trust means that people can rely on each other. When there is insufficient trust between managers and employees communication suffers badly; what is said is not believed. Trust stimulates constructive relationships and encourages goodwill. Self-interest, if carried to extremes, is destructive to organizations. Trust cannot be manufactured by deception; managers will only be trusted if they behave in trustworthy ways.

Trust is based on managers being honest, consistent, realistic, following-through and acting fairly and decently. Trust is based on a personal decison. It is built when leaders behave with integrity and principle. Once destroyed, trust can only be rebuilt with painful slowness.

Another cause of inadequate communication has been recognized by psychologists but frequently overlooked by managers, as it is insidious and pervasive. We call the problem 'prejudice'.

People can be disposed to treat other groups or individuals as inferiors. Such prejudiced attitudes cause major communication problems. Healthy communities are based on the principle of fairness. The most common kinds of prejudice are racial, sexual, religious and between social classes. Prejudice is destructive because it increases social distance and devalues human relationships. This is particularly damaging because prejudice is often energized by aggression and hostility. Disadvantaged groups, once they begin to organize and protest, present big problems for managers. Energy is swallowed up by conflict. Unfairness undermines unity. Organizations which are fragmented by social class differences experience particular difficulties. Groups can and do take traditional roles and show allegiance to their class rather than to the whole organization.

Organizations function better when they create a family feeling. Japanese executives will make enormous efforts to engender a spirit of caring. They see it as important, for each employee to feel recognized. Perhaps the most relevant technique in this area is 'team building'.

Teamwork is essential in healthy communities. Not only does it give people a sense of personal worth but it also provides the support needed to share ideas, agree objectives, develop plans and use others' strengths. Supportive teamwork requires respect for difference. People play distinct roles in teams. All the different contributions must be co-ordinated by a skilled leader who can build an effective team from a disparate group of individuals. Teams must avoid destructive games. Negative relationships destroy teamwork by undermining the quality of human support and generating defensiveness.

Decision making

Those who take decisions about the future of the organization are in a vulnerable position. Their power is formidable but the risks of error are profound. In order to take wise decisons top managers need information to be gathered like the best battlefield intelligence is gathered.

Top management must have communication from below. Intelligence must be gathered so that potential problems and opportunities are well understood.

An upward flow of communication is vital for five reasons: to collect information about strengths, weaknesses, opportunities and threats; to harvest ideas and creativity; to take the temperature of the organization; to be open to challenge and to be seen to be responsive.

There are three principal methods of gathering data from below: by channelling information upwards through the management hierarchy; by direct contact between senior managers and people on the 'shopfloor' and through surveys. Channels of decision making and upward communication can become slow and inefficient with much unnecessary communication taking place. Tortuous and wasteful communication is 'red tape' and it consumes much time and generates frustration. 'Red tape' must be fought and defeated but, like the weeds in the garden, it easily grows again!

Different types of organization have their own kinds of red tape. Simple organizations, reporting to one manager, rarely have elaborate systems. However, larger organizations which are ruled by procedures can become encumbered by stultifying disciplines. Those organizations which give a professional service can become particularly disintegrated and difficult to manage. Many large organizations have been broken down into separate operating divisions as an antidote to excessive red tape. However, red tape is most destructive in creative organizations which are trying to push back the frontiers of knowledge or technology.

Individual communication skills, both spoken and written, are the foundation of effective organizational communications. Individuals must be able to express themselves effectively otherwise mistakes occur, opportunities are missed, and poor decisions are taken.

Communication skills include accurate self perception, assertion, active listening, leadership, methodical approaches to problem solving and decision making, counselling, dealing with unconstructive people, trainer competence, creativity, writing skills and oral communication competence. Effective communication ensures that:

- People at all levels are sensitive to changes in the outside environment
- Top management gives inspiration and direction
- Managers are skilful persuaders
- The work of specialists is well integrated
- All possible steps are taken to overcome geographical barriers
- Everyone knows what is required from them
- Those with power are trusted
- No group is treated as inferior because of prejudice
- People support each other in teams

- There is an effective upward flow of communication
- Communication processes are speedy and cost-effective
- Individuals are skilled in personal communication skills
-

Key concepts

- Organizations need a 'vision of the future'
- The vision must be shared by all who hold power and communicated to the rest of the organization
- Managers need skills of persuasion
- Communication integrates the work of different departments, functions and people
- Physical layout affects communications
- Downward communication is an essential integrating force.
- Insufficient trust and prejudice inhibit communication
- Communication from below is a necessary ingredient of wise decision making
- 'Red tape' is most destructive in organizations which need to be creative
- Individual communication skills are the foundation of effective organizational communication
- Communication skills include accurate self-perception, assertion, active listening, leadership and methodical decision making and counselling, dealing with unconstructive people, trainer competence, creativity, writing and oral skills.

Blockage 12 – Poor teamwork

'United we stand,
divided we fall.'
Aesop

Organizations exist to do complex tasks that no individual could handle alone. One man could never have reached the moon unaided or sold Coca-Cola throughout the world. Working together in groups is enjoyable and personally satisfying for most people. Together, a team can accomplish much more than the total individual efforts of its own members.

All teams have a tendency to follow certain rules. When a team is well led and meets the needs of its members, it channels great energy into effective work. On the other hand, a badly led team that frustrates its members expends a great deal of productive energy grumbling and retaliating.

People quickly recognize poor teamwork: the job never gets done properly, and bickering and lethargy develop among teammates. A poor management team results in widespread evils – chiefly, unhelpful competition, lack of integration, forgotten objectives, and a sullen sense of the impossibility of making progress.

Recently we conducted a team review. The comments of team members provide a vivid impression of what can go wrong when a team is working ineffectively.

- We lacked fundamental disciplines
- The issues weren't really understood
- We didn't consider how to organize
- Time constraints were ignored

- Roles weren't clarified
- We didn't identify what we had to be good at in order to succeed
- We jumped into action
- Interdependencies were not considered
- Did not consider all the options available
- Failed to collect all the information
- Lacked a person to control the team's process.

Building a team is the result of much careful development by an overseer of the group. A supervisor must 'tend' his team with considerable effort and care. Like gardening, building a team involves responding to the seasons, meeting the needs of each 'plant', and keeping the balance of the whole in mind.

This is recognized by the most talked-about managers of all – the sports-team managers – who put tremendous effort into creating a climate in which each player is respected and still focuses all energies on the team's performance. The effect of such efforts by teammates is to multiply the resourcefulness of the team many times. In the hands of a brilliant manager, who knows how to utilize the talents of a group, a no-chance, second-rate team can topple first-rate giants and be the best of the best.

Robert Townsend, author of *Up the Organization,*[1] tells this story about his first day as the new chief executive of Avis, which had been consistently losing money in the past. The outgoing chief executive told Townsend that he would first have to fire all his managers. Three years later, the company had made ten million dollars – but with exactly the same people.

Almost everyone finds themselves a member of a group which fails to identify or achieve its objectives. Group relations are frequently lifeless, defensive, ineffective, unsatisfying and confusing. This is a costly defect in any organization since much planning and decision making depends not just on individuals but also on group effectiveness. Managing change in a turbulent environment requires that people come together to co-ordinate resources, initiate and progress ideas, gain commitment to common goals and collectively manage complex operations.

Many managers claim to favour and practise a team approach but few have a clear understanding of what this means in practice. Only in recent years have we clearly diagnosed the characteristics of effective working groups and learned to express them in down-to-earth terms. It is now possible for a manager to develop the skills which will enable him deliberately and logically to build a team out of a dispirited and unco-ordinated collection of individuals.

Teambuilding is a conscious and deliberate process to develop the kind of group which consistently achieves good results. This implies that group effectiveness is important and that there is a task to be accomplished which requires that people work together to ensure success. The development of an effective team can be compared with the growth of a child from infancy to adulthood. There are many steps to maturity which cannot be exactly predicted but the overall process usually goes through well-defined stages.

When a team is working well it is a creative and resourceful unit. The team has been described as 'the most powerful tool known to man'. It has the capacity to generate a uniquely stimulating, supporting and energetic climate which is enjoyed and valued by individuals and also generates achievement of a high order. Managers develop teams for several reasons.

- Team management is a positive and effective style where authoritarian approaches are no longer acceptable
- Teams motivate and sustain their members and energize people towards achievement
- Teams can be developed into creative problem-solving units which harness multidisciplinary skills
- Speedy decisions are possible using a team approach
- Complete tasks are competently dealt with
- Interpersonal difficulties, confusion over roles and inadequate performance are issues which are more likely to be resolved in a team.

However, the team approach is not a panacea for all management problems. It offers a useful tool for managing groups which have the potential to work together and accomplish common tasks. A 'team' may be defined as a group of people who directly relate together to achieve shared objectives. The need for direct relationships must be real and this effectively limits team approaches to groups with no more than ten or so members. Modified team approaches have been developed for large and less integrated groups. The case for teambuilding is potent. Many working groups are responsible for planning, innovation and sustaining a high level of output, yet they fail to use the ability and competence of individual members.

Some managers just seem to have a knack for building their people into an energetic, working team; others create mean and dull groups that avoid facing issues and that spend precious time backbiting and passing the buck. A manager may not realize what is valuable or destructive, but the process of building better work teams can be learned.

Successful team leaders are, above all, true to themselves, clear about standards, yet willing to give great trust and loyalty to the team, even during rough times. Also they have the personal strength to maintain the integrity and position of the unit. Especially important is the need to be receptive to people's needs, and to pay attention to their hopes and dignity.

Because many people cannot fight authority successfully, the style a manager adopts is a very important factor. Those of us who are responsible for leading teams have to make a serious choice about the way we manage, because whatever style we choose should reflect a deeply held personal belief. People quickly detect any attempt at role playing.

When we look at a management team, or at any other group or committee, there are two aspects of effectiveness that are more important than anything else: facing facts and establishing sound procedures.

Stages of working

We have found that people go through the following stages in facing situations and developing their groups.

Initial wariness

During this stage, personal feelings, weaknesses and mistakes are covered up, and people are careful not to offer views that are contrary to the established line. No one cares much about others' views and there is no shared understanding about what needs to be done.

If the group remains at this stage, there is an increase in

paperwork and in bureaucracy, people confine themselves to their own jobs, and the team manager, not knowing what else to do, rules with a firmer hand. This may work satisfactorily if the manager has the wisdom, energy and time to make the necessary decisions, but it is not teamwork in the real sense.

A sorting-out process

If the members of the group, especially the team manager, want to face problems more openly, for the purpose of improvement and not punishment, then the group evolves toward a deeper level of working. People watch carefully to see whether they are punished for being bold. If problems can be discussed openly and without rancour, the group may become rather inward-looking and group members become concerned about the views and problems of their colleagues.

In this stage, the team becomes open, but without further development it will remain somewhat inept, without the capacity to act in a unified, economic and effective way.

Self-organization

The group now has the confidence and trust in itself to take a fresh, rigorous look at how it operates and to devise new procedures for functioning more effectively. A more systematic, open approach develops which involves working through problems in a clear, energetic, and methodical way. Each of the following steps is followed in making decisions.

- *Clarifying the purpose.* It has been said that a true fanatic redoubles his effort when he loses sight of his reason for action. We should never get so involved with the mechanics of working that we lose sight of our purpose. Effective teams are somewhat cynical, frequently asking, 'What is this really going to do for us?'
- *Establishing the objective.* It is one of the clichés of our era that objectives are important. Although thousands of managers have witnessed the demise of management-by-objectives schemes under a soft cushion of red tape and empty phrases, managers must assign priorities and establish objectives for themselves in order to be really effective.

- *Collecting information.* Decisions are made on the basis of information, opinion, and intuition. Experience painfully teaches us that if objective information precedes a decision, it is more likely to be a good one. This is part of the managerial trade. Just as a woodworker knows what has to be done to make a cabinet, so a successful manager knows what information is necessary to make a sound decision.
- *Considering the options.* Generally, there are various ways of responding to a situation. When a group can generate all of its possible options before making a decision, the action will likely be more appropriate.
- *Detailed planning.* Although it may seem expedient to act quickly, skipping the planning stage can lead to a great deal of wasted effort. Professional specialists exist to assist an organization in planning its work, but the fact remains that planning is an important skill that should not be subcontracted.
- *Reviewing from experience.* Experience is one of the great teachers, but as someone pointed out, both the best and the worst flute players in the world learned their skills from experience. Practice or experience alone does not make perfect, but learning from experience can.

The mature team

After the 'self-organization' stage has developed, there is a basis for a really mature team, with flexibility from a sound foundation as the keynote. Leadership is decided by the needs of the situation rather than by protocol, and energies are used for the benefit of the team as a whole.

Further, at this stage of development the team is concerned with thinking through the basic principles and responsibilities of management, including commercial, economic, and social aspects.

It is also necessary to make plans for the continual development of the group, recognizing that we live in a changing world in which inactivity inevitably means sterility and decay.

We believe that all individuals and groups are capable of development. The investment of time and effort in purposefully developing teamwork results in a very precious resource - being able to work together. The success of any enterprise depends on this ability.

However, many potential teams fail to develop as effective units. This largely results from managers being unaware of the benefits of teamwork and unskilled in the techniques of developing effective working groups. When a team is working well it is a highly resourceful, energetic unit which sustains individual morale and combines differing personal strengths into a powerful group. The word synergy has been coined to describe this special blend of energy and competence.

An effective team will show the following characteristics:

- It will establish and work towards clear objectives
- It will have open relationships between members
- It will deal with different viewpoints and gain from debate
- Members will show a high level of support for each other
- Personal relationships will be based on personal knowledge and trust
- People will want to work together to get things done
- Potentially damaging conflicts will be worked through and resolved
- Procedures and decision-making processes will be effective
- Leadership will be skilful and appropriate to the needs of the team
- It will regularly review its operations and try to learn from experiences
- Individuals will be developed and the team will be capable of dealing with strong and weak personalities
- Relations with other groups will be co-operative and open.

The organization which fails to develop the competence of its teams loses an important resource. Organizations which identify the need to develop team competence must also convince everyone concerned of the potential value of teamwork, and provide the necessary skills and support to enable teambuilding to take place.

Key concepts

- Teamwork is vital to organizational effectiveness

- The quality of team leadership is the most significant factor
- Poor teamwork is inefficient, frustrating and wasteful
- Teams can be deliberately built
- A well-developed team motivates its members and enhances creativity
- The team leader must pay attention to the different individual needs of each member
- Teams go through four stages of development: initial wariness, sorting out, self-organization and maturity
- Mature teams are open and trustworthy
- Team competence begins with a commitment to people.

Reference

1.   Robert Townsend, *Up the Organization,* Fawcett, New York, 1970.

Blockage 13 – Low motivation

> 'If men define situations as real,
> they are real in their consequences.'
> Robert K. Merton

Successful army generals, football team managers, school teachers and political leaders all understand the importance of people being committed to the task in hand.

The ability to do a particular job is one thing, but wanting to do it is quite another. History is full of situations where people have succeeded in achieving a particular goal, despite almost impossible odds, when they really wanted to.

Although different kinds of leadership are relevant to accomplishing various tasks, especially important is the ability to find the right keys to unlock the latent energy in people and to harness it to the task at hand. This is an important skill, one that depends on a leader's wisdom and emotions; but when this skill is used well and when people feel the importance of a particular action, they will make considerable efforts to achieve success.

Unfortunately, managers rarely consider the way people feel about the organization of their work. Rebellion, resistance, malice and lack of interest are common throughout the world.

Managers must understand what motivates their subordinates. This is never standardized.

Motivators vary greatly but we have found that there are nine distinct motivators:

1. *Material rewards:* seeking possession, wealth and a high standard of living. Material rewards are defined as tangible assets, including money, possessions, quality of housing, and

other material possessions.

People with material rewards as a motivator take decisions about future work life primarily to enhance their material wellbeing. They seek roles which provide a high income and they take on tasks which may be unfulfilling or uncongenial but which provide that high income or other material rewards.

The key concern in this motivator is wealth.

2. *Power/Influence:* seeking to be in control of people and resources. Power/influence is defined as wanting to be dominant and to have others behave in subordinate roles. Also connected is wanting to take decisions about policy and how resources are expended.

People who have power/influence as a motivator gravitate towards managerial or political roles. They are proactive, they use personal power, and they have high self-confidence and clear ideas about what should be done. They are concerned with impact.

The key concern in this motivator is dominance.

3. *Search for meaning:* seeking to do things which are believed valuable for their own sake. Search for meaning is defined as being motivated to do things considered to be a contribution to something bigger, finer or greater than the individual according to religious, emotional, moral, social or intellectual criteria.

People with the search for meaning as a motivator will take decisions which are explicable only in the context of their personal beliefs and values. This may take the form of helping others rather than helping themselves. Personal fulfilment is the ultimate payoff, and they may make considerable sacrifices in order to follow their inner beliefs.

The key concern in this motivator is contribution.

4. *Expertise:* seeking a high level of accomplishment in a specialized field. Expertise is defined as specialist knowledge, skills, knowhow, competence and capacity to perform unusual, difficult or specialized activities.

People with expertise as a motivator work hard to gain a depth of competence in limited but specified fields and will strive to maintain their specialist capability. They dislike going outside their defined area. One of their primary sources of satisfaction is being valued as an expert. The expertise may be mechanical, craft, intellectual, scientific or practical. Professional managers can be included in this category, especially those with formal training in management sciences.

The key concern in this motivator is mastery.

5. *Creativity:* seeking to innovate and be identified with original output. Creativity is here defined as devising something new which bears the name of the originator. This may be a work of science, art, literature, research, architecture; an entrepreneurial activity or even a form of entertainment.

People with creativity as a motivator do things which are distinctly different from those which others do, and they want to own the results. The individual's name is closely associated with his or her products. Genuine innovation is very highly prized.

People driven by creativity derive excitement from breaking new ground. They are stimulated by puzzles, riddles, challenges and problems. They can tolerate setbacks or failures without letting them destroy optimism. A feeling of accomplishment in producing something novel is a vital element.

The key concern in this motivator is originality.

6. *Affiliation:* seeking nourishing relationships with others. Affiliation is defined as striving to be close to others, enjoying bonds of friendship and being enriched by human relationships.

People who have affiliation as a motivator take initiatives to develop deep and fulfilling relationships with others. These bonds become extremely important to them. They put their feelings for others above self-aggrandizement and preserve continuity in important relationships. They may continue with unsatisfactory or unfulfilling jobs because of the quality of their relationships with others. Their commitment is to people, not to task, position or organizational goals.

The key concern in this motivator is closeness.

7. *Autonomy:* seeking to be independent and able to make decisions for oneself. Autonomy is defined as taking personal responsibility for the structure, processes and objectives of

daily life.

People with autonomy as a motivator act to increase the amount of control they have over their own working lives. They resist attempts by organizations to put them in boxes. They identify, and then fight, constraints. People like this often fail to cope well with bureaucracy and seek to become their own masters. They enjoy feeling 'I did it all', and they prefer to work alone or with a small team which they lead.

The desire for independence is very influential in autonomy-driven individuals. They do not like to be directed by others. They experience the procedures, systems, conventions and protocols of others as irritants.

The key concern in this motivator is choice.

8. *Security:* seeking a solid and predictable future. Security is defined as wanting to know the future and to avoid being exposed to unpredictable risks.

People with security as a motivator take decisions which help them to feel relaxed about their future. Their primary goal is high predictability, rather than high income. They see life as a journey to be undertaken by the safest routes with the best maps and guides available.

This type of person chooses employers after careful consideration of their stability and record of looking after employees. They may associate security with membership of blue chip companies or institutions. They make career choices with the future in mind. If a promotion opportunity substantially increases doubt about the future, they may well reject it. People driven by security accept what the world has to offer rather than taking a radical stance.

The key concern in this motivator is assurance.

9. *Status:* seeking to be recognized, admired and respected by the community at large. Status is defined as wanting the esteem of others, and to be highly regarded. Status is demonstrated by symbols, formal recognition and acceptance into privileged groups.

People with status as a motivator undertake whatever actions are needed in order to enhance their prestige. This includes making personal contacts with influential people, taking responsible assignments and self-publicizing. They may seek positions of power and authority, but their desire is for the prestige of the position rather than the exercise of control.

The key concern in this motivator is position.

Motives are influenced by the wider culture. The factors which drive a New York financier are quite different from an Islamic fundamentalist mullah.

Expectations can also change between generations. Two or three generations ago it was accepted, without question, that work was a necessary part of life. Students at universities diligently attended classes in suits and ties and groomed themselves for a career in industry. Today, much has changed, and many more options are available. The principles of our fathers are increasingly questioned. Some organizations have adapted to the expectations of the new generation, but not without conflict and stress.

If an employee feels alienated from his place of work, then he or she has not entered into a meaningful 'contract' and will invest only the minimum energy to perform an assigned task.

One method of determining our worth to our employers is by the amount of cash we receive at the end of the week. Many managers feel that this is by far the most important factor and that everything else is irrelevant or 'soft soap'. But cash is not everything; there are other ways of showing an individual's worth.

Consider the person living on welfare benefits. Even though he or she may receive adequate cash, without meaningful work there is a loss of self-value and esteem.

Many may not agree, but evidence confirms that quality of work itself is as important to most people as their wage, provided that they are not consumed by passionate grievances about being underpaid. As the influence of money as a driving force declines, psychological rewards become more significant. (However, see also Blockage 8 – Unfair rewards.)

Work not only occupies a large proportion of our lifetime, it also occupies those hours when we are at our brightest. The stake we all have in our working lives is immense, and many feel that it is one of the tragedies of our times that so many people have lost the feeling that their work is, in any way, meaningful.

According to Frederick Herzberg,[1] an American psychologist who has worked extensively on problems of motivation, if you ask people what satisfied them most in their working lifetime, more often than not they will tell you about some tricky aspect of their job that they managed to do well. In other words, their satisfaction came from achievement rather than from payment, clean lavatories, or a company outing, the things that managers usually provide in an attempt to satisfy the needs of employees.

There are two important lessons to be learned from Herzberg's research.

* We often assume that we know other people's needs, but we are frequently wrong
* The financial and welfare practices that a company follows are important, but they do not, by themselves, motivate people to improve.

Motivation problems are not standardized. For example, demotivators for people performing routine tasks include:

* job boredom
* feeling that they have little prospects of advancement
* financial rewards tend to be below average
* high performers are rarely recognized or rewarded
* tasks lack meaning
* decisions are taken by those above, but often not explained
* individuals fail to receive feedback on their performance.

In a non-routine environment motivation problems are very different. Issues may include:

* frequent short time-scale tasks overloading people
* routine work imposed on highly ambitious people
* new objectives meaning that effort is sometimes wasted
* lack of clarity about roles and contributions
* too many decision makers reducing individual autonomy
* 'political' factors proving more important than rational argument, hence a feeling of unfairness.

Managing technical people often brings its own motivational problems:

* insufficient workload, especially if work is boring
* perception that pay is uncompetitive
* lack of recognition by immediate management
* mismatch of skills with tasks
* remote leadership style

- excessively authoritarian management style
- inconsistent leadership values
- inappropriate work measurement systems
- excessive bureaucracy (red tape)
- lack of clear downward communication to specify and explain objectives
- insufficient investment in training
- underdeveloped technology or systems
- insecurity bred by lack of communication.

Fortunately, motivational problems are intractable but not insoluble. Each issue can be addressed, but this is never easy. Motivational problems must be individually diagnosed, isolated, and tackled as a whole.

Motivating an organization cannot be driven just from the top. Managers and supervisors right through the organization need to be part of an overall planned effort to create and sustain a motivating climate. This requires a continuing programme of training to develop team leader skills and to bring about the right attitudes. High motivation is never accidental; it is a result of sustained commitment and diligent effort.

Creating and sustaining a motivating climate requires that senior management really cares about people. Attempts to sustain high motivation will fail without a deep commitment to the feelings of employees. Motivation is about energy, excitement, vitality, commitment and satisfaction. In the last analysis motivation is a result of an individual finding *meaning* in his or her job.

Leaders who are great motivators are never impersonal, dull or bland. They understand that the essence of leadership is obtaining a consensus on a common vision. This vision can include profitability, but mere financial gain is insufficient to attract many people. Vision needs to tap into individual values and become an opportunity for self-expression for each employee.

People find meaning in different activities according to their personality, position in life, self-image and so on. There are many motivators. One man may seek to find spiritual truth as a hermit incarcerated in a remote cave in the Sahara Desert, whilst another is driven by the possession of status, wealth and power as a captain of industry. Despite the incredible variety of human motivations there are common characteristics that motivate most people. It is these common motivational features that managers must identify and resolve.

A motivation improvement programme must develop pride in the firm, in the job and in the product. Close links with the customer helps.

Routine environments require rules, but constraints must be accepted by the employer. It is important to bring 'fun' into the workplace. A strong team spirit helps to provide an antidote to the dehumanization of the workplace. Within the team context, clear attainable goals help to ensure that each person feels a sense of pride as a master of his or her trade. Constant innovation is necessary to inject energy and commitment into the routine organization. Ways must be found to encourage competition, reward and recognition. Feedback on performance is critical, with praise given whenever it is earned. Somehow management should find ways for people to feel special. It is no accident that well motivated groups feel themselves to be an elite.

Project environments require a different motivational framework. Specialists need to give a measure of freedom to innovate. Encouragement of risk taking develops autonomy. This is especially true of innovative environments which require a strong sense of vision. Complete openness is essential, and again teamwork is key.

High vs. low motivation

It is commonly observed that a highly motivated person puts care and energy into the job. Where the opposite is the case, a dull, negative, and even destructive reaction is often present.

If we have a need and we satisfy it, then it ceases to be a need. Take air, for example. Usually we do not feel a need for air because it exists plentifully everywhere. But if we are caught underwater and are unable to breathe, then the desire for air becomes the most important need in our existence. The same is generally true for food and drink, warmth, sex, and all other physiological needs.[2]

When basic physical needs are fulfilled, people generally seek their social needs - security, affection, family, and social position. After this stage, man seeks higher aims - the recognition and activation of his own potential and the search to find deeper meaning in life.

Human drive and energy result when individuals strive to satisfy their needs. If a company provides an environment fostering satisfaction, it will enable people to meet their needs.

A company that frustrates employees is usually characterized by low motivation. Visitors can sense the lack of life and atmosphere as soon as they walk through the door – workers may seem 'switched off' and involved in their own private worlds. Even though some work is being done, it is performed as a drudgery. The visitor may feel that if he stood at the exit at one minute to five, he would likely be injured in the rush to escape.

In summary, motivation is a question of energy and commitment. We all have untapped sources of energy that are not expressed because we do not see the value of committing ourselves. If we work for an organization that recognizes our worth and gives due weight and dignity to the time we spend working, then we will, naturally, give more of ourselves in return. This helps make the experience of working more fulfilling for each employee and more profitable for the organization.

Key concepts

- Creating and sustaining a motivating climate is a primary leadership task
- There are nine basic motivators: material rewards, power/ influence, search for meaning, expertise, creativity, affiliation, autonomy, security and status
- Motivation is both cultural and individual
- Meaning and challenge are the real motivators at work
- Different organizations have particular motivational problems related to the nature of work processes
- High motivation is never accidental: it results from commitment and effort
- It is important to bring vision and fun into the workplace
- A climate which recognizes and praises success is motivating for most people
- High motivation is essential if the organization is to provide quality, care and innovation for its customers.

References

1. Frederick Herzberg, *Work and the nature of man*, New American Library, New York, 1973.
2. A.H. Maslow, (ed.) *Motivation and personality*, 2nd ed., Harper and Row, New York, 1970.

Blockage 14 - Low creativity

'We have come to the point in biological history where we are now responsible for our own evolution.'
Abraham Maslow

There was a time not so long ago when it was necessary to learn only one trade or profession in a lifetime, and the knowledge and skills a man acquired in his youth were still relevant on his retirement day. This, however, is no longer the situation. Some industries, like electronics engineering, face a continual and often bewildering rate of change that demands constant effort to keep up with the current practices. Many other trades are less influenced by change, but only a few are totally free of innovation (horse breaking and dog training are the only ones we can think of on the spur of the moment).

Organizations and individuals live in a world of constant flux that comes from numerous sources - politics, society, education, technology; the list is virtually endless. Any organization that wishes to survive and grow needs to keep up with these trends and changes.

Consider the patterns of our economy. There is a decline in the number of people employed in manufacturing and an increase in the number employed in service industries. There is a move towards mass production and mass marketing. Products are less permanent, and some designs have built-in obsolescence. Jobs that are particularly dirty, hot, noisy, or unsatisfying tend to remain unfilled despite local unemployment. The smokestack economy is turning into a microchip economy. All these changes represent a challenge to our present practices; to survive we must keep ahead by generating new ideas and practices – by being creative.

True creativity depends on being in close touch with the present situation and being able to battle against all that is repetitive, mechanical and insensitive in our make-up. This demands a quality and depth of attention that is hard to achieve. The computer, which surpasses man in many ways, is a cumbersome idiot when something new has to be generated. This is the unique contribution of people – sensitivity, flexibility and creative spark. These qualities can easily be stunted and destroyed by clumsy handling, but they are fundamental to successful achievement.

In practice, creativity is often difficult to institutionalize because it challenges the established order and replaces certainty with uncertainty. Because people often fear this, you may hear comments like 'better the devil you know'. In addition, the creative person more often than not makes mistakes and is often criticized for being unable to sort out the bizarre from the practical. However, if each new idea were censored before being expressed, in all likelihood it would go through such an obstacle course that its potential value would never be known.

Because there are many forces working to inhibit creativity, we must consciously try to neutralize them and enable this untidy but vital creative process to flourish.

The uncreative organization

The uncreative organization works like a machine – either a very well-constructed and well-maintained machine or a creaking, slow and ill-designed device. Nevertheless, it is a machine, whose parts interact in completely predictable ways.

The managers spend little time developing new ideas for the future and pay only lip service to the importance of forward-looking ideas from employees. When someone does have an unusual idea, it is given a cold reception, unless it comes from the boss, whose notions are accepted without question. Others learn that it is safer not to 'rock the boat'.

People in uncreative organizations often learn that taking risks is dangerous and unrewarding. If it is the company's custom and practice to condemn every failure with gleeful malice, then people (especially managers) will be scared to do anything that involves uncertainty. As a result, managers stop having new ideas.

This can take root at every level. For top managers, it means that decisions about finance, marketing and products are excessively conservative, protracted and half-hearted. At lower levels, no one seems concerned to reorganize the stockroom or to simplify a particular document.

The effect of such creative constipation is the likelihood that a competitor will take another jump ahead of you. Carried to extremes, the uncreative organization is a dying organization, one that has lost contact with the application and energy of its founders, that mechanically repeats old patterns, and that ceases to meet the needs of customers. Such an organization, like the dinosaur, will rapidly become extinct.

The overcreative organization

You will not find many of these, but it is worth describing what happens when creativity is taken to excess.

Sometimes there is such a high value placed on new ideas that people spend all their energy thinking them up without putting them to the test. Endless possibilities and lines of inquiry are opened up, but the ideas stay at a rather rarefied and abstract level, and no one knows how to get things moving. Eventually, the organization collapses into impotence because it cannot choose between its many possibilities.

How to be creative

Creativity is a delicate plant – more like an orchid than a cabbage – which needs the right atmosphere and conditions to flourish. In an organic environment new ideas and risk taking are welcome and rewarded.

Initially, there is a need to break away from old habits and routines and to extend our range of thinking so that all sorts of unconnected ideas can come together in unpredictable ways. The surfeit of ideas that often results must then be evaluated, selected and developed.

Applying new ideas, like creating them, is a test of management competence. Even a brilliant thought must be developed and used before it becomes valuable.

Lack of creative capacity can seriously undermine organizational effectiveness. Some managers believe creative ability is very thinly distributed among the population. This view is, in itself, uncreative. Creativity is constantly expressed by people in all walks of life.

There are two primary approaches to increasing creative capacity. The first is to consider what psychological barriers could be blocking personal creative capacity. The second is to examine how you can systematically apply creative methods to solving problems in your organization.

Barriers to personal creativity

Once you recognize that you have much more capacity than you use, then the next, and major, part of your personal development requires you to identify and reduce the inner barriers that are blocking your natural ability.

We have identified seven important factors that have blocked or limited our own creativity or that of our friends.

Laziness

Creativity takes time and effort. Giving up prematurely prevents barriers to creative accomplishment from being broken down. Discipline is needed to assign time to creative effort and sometimes boredom has to be endured. Genuine difficulties and apparently insoluble problems often occur with creative tasks but the difficult stages of creativity can be experienced and survived, if you do not succumb to laziness.

Traditional habits

All people develop routines of movement, work, expression and thinking, but habits can be enemies of creativity. Traditional habits should be examined, and the question 'Why?' is a powerful tool for that task. By going back to first principles, reviewing the processes of thought that seemed logical in the past, you can decide whether they continue to be effective.

Excessive tension

Being creative often involves feelings of uncertainty and confusion. Almost by definition, you do not know the answer before you begin, and this lack of a secure foundation can provoke excessive tension in some people. They experience such tension both physically and emotionally, responding as though they were defending themselves against physical danger. Rigid responses and sensations of pressure and stress inhibit the emotional and imaginative leaps of the creative process. People who are tense try to cling to solid realities and in the process they limit their energies. Both factors hamper creative effort.

Muted drive

It has been said that no significant development occurs without the existence of a felt requirement for change. Creative endeavours are fuelled by a desire for change. The need to innovate can be initiated in the individual or from an external situation. For example, recent wars have stimulated fantastic feats in fields as diverse as brain surgery, espionage, photography and journalism. To be creative, it is necessary for people to feel a need to change, recognizing the limitations of old processes and wanting to find better alternatives.

Insufficient opportunity

Some of the most significant innovations in hisotry were conceived by individuals prevented from conducting their lives normally through such limitations as illness, imprisonment, or even temporary disgrace. For many people, a normal life means filling their days with routines that consume the vast majority of their time and energy; their opportunities for innovation are few. For others, their chosen forms of creativity require external resources and support. If these are lacking, it becomes virtually impossible to collect the necessary data or to structure experiments. This requires personal assertion which is an essential component in creative action because the allocation of time, energy, resources and support are vital components in the creative process.

Over-seriousness

Creative expression often requires a willingness to play with ideas; sometimes solutions lie with bizarre and extraordinary suggestions. This playful receptivity is not compatible with excessive seriousness and an obsessive concern with rationality. The lack of a playful attitude also inhibits communication with others. The excitement of a new idea brings vitality, but over-serious responses can sap ideas of their strength, making it difficult for others to become enthused.

Poor methodology

The lack of an appropriate and effective method of problem solving inhibits creative effort. Although, by definition, creative work involves novel thinking, it is possible to find ways of structuring such work to increase the probability of success. The creative process can be examined and analysed in the same way as other aspects of management functioning and it is possible to acquire skills and develop methods that assist in this.

Creativity in organizations

The history of innovation is marked by significant breakthroughs made by famous people of undoubted genius: Newton's gravitational theory, Einstein's relativity, the Wrights' powered flight, Land's instant camera, etc. People become accustomed to thinking of creativity as a personal and eccentric capacity – a gift that, somehow, particular individuals possess.

However, a deeper examination of innovative progress shows that much has been achieved by organizations or communities. Their creative accomplishments have often been a consequence of the pooled talent of many people. Although certain individuals have been highlighted for their contributions, they could not have achieved the end results alone. A team or organization nourished the creative output, giving individuals the resources and backup they needed. The American and Soviet space programmes are excellent examples of organizational innovation, but history is full of similar cases. Wells Cathedral, the computer and the space shuttle are all products of the creative imaginations of many individuals.

An individual can handle the creative work of a limited project, but when the scale of the task becomes large and complicated creative teams have to be formed. Although the capability to interact with data-handling electronic machines can increase an individual's ability to manage complex problems, there comes a point when individual brilliance is not the answer. Not only do the limitations of intellectual capacity prevent large-scale projects from being accomplished by individuals, but enthusiasm, energy, morale and courage are also needed. The active support of others does much to sustain the individual while the frustrating development and execution of ideas are being undertaken. Almost everyone has talents that can be harnessed to help a team be more innovative, but individual abilities must be recognized and appreciated before they can be put to use. It is, therefore, necessary for members of a creative group to learn about one another's skills, knowledge and potential contributions.

A creative group requires a balance of skills and capacities. For example, a production team will need people to translate design concepts into operational plans, to match technical and organizational ability, and to combine marketing flair with solid research work. Leadership is an important factor in the group's success because the manager will want to build a resourceful and balanced group that contains a broad mixture of talents. The creative group should include a spread of relevant technical skills and also a range of personality types to give it balance and energy.

The role of leader of a creative group deserves to be explored in depth. There are those who believe that leadership is a permanent and unchanging attribute possessed by some lucky mortals from birth, but this is far from the truth. Leadership is learned and leadership styles must change according to the demands of the situation and the maturity of the group being managed. A creative team presents special problems to its manager, problems that stem from the following conditions:

1. *Unclear objectives.* Creative groups may lack clear objectives, their tasks may be imprecise and the utility of their output may only be evaluated after its completion.
2. *Insufficient support.* Because organizations are notorious for withdrawing support from creative groups, there is a need for such a group to communicate, gain acceptance and ensure material support.
3. *Unco-ordinated activity.* When searching for solutions or ideas, individual activity is often unco-ordinated. As a result, a situation can quickly develop in which all the group members are engaged in duplication and unsystematic initiatives.
4. *Loss of heart.* Snags and setbacks can occur as a project proceeds. They can seriously demoralize the participants and lead to a collapse of the group's initiative and energy.
5. *Communication overload.* Creative teams need to communicate extensively and the process of discussion clarifies issues. However, too much data can overload the system, preventing key topics from being identified.
6. *Inadequate review.* As new data are generated, a task changes in character and scope. Because it is not easy to stay open to change, continuing to work on outdated guidelines can be tempting. This temptation should be counteracted by review and replanning for creative endeavours.

The manager responsible for a creative group will have to watch for these potential pitfalls and plan to remedy them should they occur. There are no foolproof answers and the manager must identify and discuss each problem with the group concerned. The group members are most likely to grant their commitment and support to solutions they have proposed and accepted. The primary task of the manager is identifying and raising issues of effectiveness, rather than supplying answers.

The creative process

People who think that being creative requires them to exceed their usual boundaries and operate on a higher level of effectiveness tend to strain in an effort to concentrate on pulling the best from themselves. Instead, they achieve the opposite effect, because creative capacity is diminished by strain and undermined by forced concentration.

Some of the clearest insights into the nature of creativity have come from recent training breakthroughs in the world of sport. There are two aspects of the human personality. One aspect, known as self one, is always judging, commenting, criticising, and being preoccupied with success and output. Another aspect of the personality, known as self two, is intuitively capable and much more in tune with the rhythm of life. As soon as a person begins to play tennis (or any other sport), the voice of self one begins to monitor the performance and to interfere with the natural capacity of self two. Thus, the dominance of one part of the personality can hinder a performance that is within a person's natural capacity.

This powerful idea is readily applicable to creative undertakings. An individual may approach a problem with preconceived expectations, fail to be fully aware of the task or the changing factors and try to hurry toward a solution. While working on the assignment, the person can be sapped of strength by a stream of doubts, criticisms and strain. It is not surprising that true creativity, which is a subtle human attribute, fails to thrive under such a hostile regime.

All innovation contains an element of risk but, in a changing world, the failure to innovate is also risky. Risks are inevitable. They also are frightening and people often invest considerable energy in trying to minimize risks, sometimes to the point of starving imagination. The results can be low achievement, ponderous decision making and frustrations.

In many ways, it is much easier to devise logical systems and to programme people to work within them than to be truly creative, open and flexible. Creativity takes courage. Yet both creativity and order are necessary; the problem is one of balance and relationship. The organization must respect both the creative and the routine, to enable both to flourish, and to provide them with ways of interrelating for the benefit of the whole.

Key concepts

- A lack of creative capacity can seriously undermine organizational effectiveness
- Today's organizations must be creative to survive
- Creativity requires creating a non-mechanistic organizational form
- Creativity is difficult to manage as it challenges the status quo
- Fear is perhaps the greatest inhibitor of creativity
- Some organizations are excessively creative and stultified as a result
- There are seven typical blockages to creativity: laziness, traditional habits, excessive tension, muted drive, insufficient opportunity, over-seriousness and poor methodology
- Creative groups require a balance of skills and abilities
- Creative teams require a high order of process skills
- Managers are well advised to study recent research into the nature of the creative process
- All innovation is risk laden, but even more risky is the absence of creativity.

Part Four

APPLYING THE CONCEPTS

Six examples in practice

This chapter of the book includes selected examples of the experiences organizations have had with the 'unblocking your organization' approach. They demonstrate ways in which ideas and materials presented in this book have been applied in practice.

1. Workshop design for a large manufacturer

A large military-equipment manufacturer identified great technical strengths in its organization but found weaknesses in its personnel management. The firm's central training department decided to build one of their courses around the 'unblocking your organization' approach and used the following workshop design.

- Participants arrive for the programme and undertake an initial activity to get to know the other members of the group.
- Each participant completes the blockage questionnaire (see p. 31) for his or her section of the organization and the results are summarized on the flip chart.
- The blockages that are identified as primary problem areas become the agenda for the programme. Each blockage area is explained, using the summary at the end of each chapter.
- Participants are divided into small discussion groups to consider, in their own language, whether the results of the

blockage questionnaire correspond with practical experience.
- When the primary blockages have been validated, training materials are selected from the companion book, *50 Activities for Unblocking Your Organization Volume 1*, to enable participants to explore the blockages further and develop skills in clearing them.
- Each participant was given a copy of *Unblocking Your Organization* and time was set aside to read relevant chapters during the programme.
- The training process used experiential learning materials. Throughout the training phase, reference was made back to the results of the blockage questionnaire.
- The final phase of the programme related learning to each participant's own practical situation.

2.   Management styles and teamwork

The following first-person description of a consulting relationship outlines the process of consultation and presents the blockage approach as a potent tool for giving feedback on their own style on top management people. This case is similar to many consulting assignments and is written in first person for convenience.

'The general manager of a medium-sized manufacturing company was young and dynamic and had big plans for the organization. However, he felt hampered by a middle management team that he regarded as lacking in drive, initiative and motivation. He complained that because of this problem he could rarely delegate important matters and, consequently, he felt overworked himself.

'As consultant to the general manager, the adviser's brief was to help improve matters. The general manager assumed this would involve something drastic happening to his middle managers. I sat in on a couple of his management meetings and also talked to all his immediate subordinates. All of them were invited to complete the blockage questionnaire. The results of the questionnaire, backed up by my conversations and observations, showed quite clearly that:

- there was a marked difference between the views of the

general manager and those of his managers

- to a person, his managers saw the problem as inappropriate management philosophy on his part
- both he and his managers saw 'poor teamwork' and 'poor training' as second- and third-level problems.

I shared with him the issue of his management style, telling him of the questionnaire results and of my own observations, and I invited him to complete a couple of activities based on McGregor's Theory X and Theory Y which he did. That meeting must have been extremely threatening to him and I was fearful that he might not have the courage to face up to the fundamental issues involved. However, he did show that courage and he made an immediate commitment to experiment with a different way of managing.

'Over the next few weeks, the two of us had a number of meetings in which his experiences were discussed. His experimentation involved using a number of activities. The going was not easy, but gradually he began to notice that his managers were responding and behaving in a different way, although, understandably, their reactions to his new methods were initially characterized by suspicion and mistrust. After a few weeks, he had gained enough confidence to tackle the other problems, some of which, because of his actions, had already begun to improve.

'After working hours, a seminar was held in which we simply fed back to the management team the results of our investigations and invited them to discuss what action was needed. The general manager started by describing what he had tried to do about his management style and his openness set the whole tone of the seminar. The group's reaction to his description was best summed up by the production manager who commented: 'You have done your bit and now it is our turn to help you in the same way that you have helped us'.

'Long after the time the seminar was scheduled to finish, the managers were still enthusiastically planning how to tackle their teamwork and training problems. The real key to this happy assignment was the courage and determination shown by the general manager, courage that was amply rewarded by the increased contribution he received from his team. The next time I met him, he glowed with pride as he described the achievements of his team members and spoke of the 'thinking time' that he now had as the result of his increased delegation to them.'

3. A local government organization

Senior executives of a large city government wanted to identify employee morale problems. To accomplish this, the city's training-services department administered the blockage questionnaire to a random sample of nearly 200 employees over a three-month period. The sample included supervisors, clerical personnel, skilled and unskilled labour.

Statistical analysis

A statistical analysis of the results was then carried out under the following headings:

- High blockage. Blockages that have the highest number of items perceived as applicable, i.e. problem areas.
- Low blockages. Blockages with the lowest number of items perceived as applicable, i.e. strengths.
- Average. The total number of items perceived as applicable, divided by the number of individuals surveyed.
- Mode. The most frequently identified number of items perceived as applicable in each blockage area.
- Average vs. mode. In computing this average, all scores are taken into account. Thus, one or two abnormal scores can bias the average, whereas the mode indicates the most frequently selected number of items.

Conclusions

Blockages were rank ordered on the basis of a department-wide average. It was interesting that there was no significant difference found among the different occupation groups surveyed.

The survey led to a short report to key executives suggesting a programme of organizational change and training activities with maximum energy devoted to resolving primary blockages.

It was also decided that the blockage questionnaire could be used for evaluating change. Plans were made to readminister it to a random sample of employees after six months in order for comparisons to be made.

4. Teambuilding in a scattered organization

A highly successful organization had a small head office and a
large number of fairly autonomous branches. It also had a
problem common to such an organization – the managers seldom
met together. Although the firm's success was largely based on
the individual entrepreneurial drive of branch managers, it was
missing out in areas where a coordinated approach was desirable.

The organization's other needs included achieving more
mutual understanding between the head office and the branches,
identifying strengths and weaknesses across the management
team and taking steps to capitalize on the strengths and eliminate
the weaknesses.

We were given one-and-a-half days to help them in this, a
period assigned for one of the rare get-togethers. During this
period we had three objectives for the managers:

- to achieve an understanding between the head office and the
  branches
- to experiment with and practise their skills as a team and to
  look at the ways in which they manage
- to identify barriers to their effectiveness as a total
  management team, and to plan action as a result.

To meet these objectives, a programme was devised that involved
working on activities to open up and encourage a frank
discussion between the head office people, who were mainly the
most senior executives in the organization, and the branch
managers, who in some instances were not at all happy with the
actions and attitudes of their senior colleagues at the head office.

The blockage questionnaire was used to identify barriers to
effectiveness and this was followed by a more detailed look at the
highest scoring blockages.

A number of structured 'activities' were used to examine
management style and teamwork.

Action planning followed. The new insights gained from these
activities, combined with the results of the blockage questionnaire
and the other team and management-style activities, enabled the

group to identify clearly its problems and opportunities.

The seminar only began the process of change and improvement in this organization, but the participants felt that the objectives of the session had been met and they had become better equipped to look at problems in their own branches.

5. Action planning with senior managers

A medium-sized organization, manufacturing products for the building and construction market, began a comprehensive programme of training managers in problem-solving skills. Having entered a difficult market, the firm needed to manage innovation much more successfully than it had in its recent history.

The company training manager worked with one of the authors in developing relevant training and a programme of structured experiences. These were combined with closed-circuit television feedback, which adds significantly to the depth of learning.

As participants progressed through the training programme, their problem-solving and other personal skills improved and they gained new ideas on management practice. Because it is often difficult to transfer learning from a training environment to real-life working situations, we designed a training module using a series of activities focused on assessing each person's working environment and identifying how the new learning could be applied. Typically, this would be undertaken on the Thursday afternoon of a five-day Monday to Friday programme. After the module was completed, counselling skills were explained and practised with video feedback (3 hours).

Action planning module

The five-hour module on action planning used the following sequence:

1. The purpose and structure of the module are explained (10 minutes).
2. A simple model for planning change is explained, using the action-planning diagram and exploring the stages described (15 minutes):

Action planning diagram

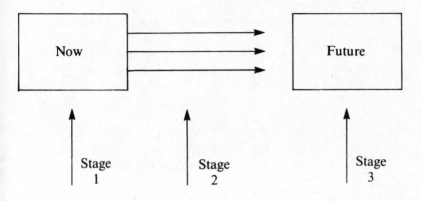

Stage 1. To get a clear diagnosis of the present situation, we should define as accurately as possible what is happening now.

Stage 2. To get a clear vision of where we would like to be and what we want to aim for, we then consider the future.

Stage 3. To manage the change between Stage 1 and Stage 2, an appropriate strategy is developed.

The action plan will be weakened if any of these steps are left out, and they must be approached with equal strength. Frequently, people reveal different strengths in these stages. Some individuals are particularly good at developing visions of the future, but find it difficult to come back to earth and analyse their present problems. Others can easily see their current difficulties, but cannot decide how the future should look.

3.   After it is explained that the initial stage will focus on the 'now' situation, the managers use the blockage questionnaire to survey their own areas. When they have completed the questionnaire, they receive a copy of this book and are asked to refer to the analysis in Part One, 'Defining organizational problems' (40 minutes).

4. All participants are asked to identify an important problem or issue on which they feel they have sufficient energy to work (5 minutes).
5. Techniques for planning change are then described.
6. Participants are asked to choose the most appropriate techniques and to use them to help with their own problems. Training staff assist during this period (35 minutes).
7. Groups of threes are formed for small-group counselling. Emphasis is placed on using counselling skills in a disciplined manner (2 hours).
8. A brief open session is held to share the participants' experiences using the techniques and the progress that has been made. Points for further exploration are emphasized (20 minutes).

6. A Hong Kong entrepreneurial company

In Hong Kong a large company sought to increase the entrepreneurial ability of divisional managers. The following process was used.

*   Each divisional manager appointed an agent (normally the personnel officer).
*   The agents were trained in test administration procedures (half-a-day).
*   The agents undertook comprehensive data collection using the blockage questionnaire. A random sample was chosen down to supervisory level.
*   The agents undertook the necessary statistical analysis breaking the data into level, function and high scored blockage questions.
*   Cluster analysis was undertaken to determine key blockages and describe their characteristics.
*   At a one-day workshop the divisional managers were given the data, and compared and contrasted their scores. Action plans were developed to unblock each organization.

Part Five

RESOURCE GUIDE

Published materials

Useful books

Adair, J. Ayres R., Debenham, I.Y., and Despres, D. (eds). *A handbook of management training exercises,* British Association for Industrial and Commercial Education, London, 1978.

Argyle, M., *Social interaction,* Methuen, London, 1969.

Argyris, C., *Integrating the individual and the organization,* John Wiley, New York, 1964.

Argyris, C., *Intervention theory and method: a behavioural science view,* Addison-Wesley, London, 1970.

Argyris, C., and Schon, D.A., *Organizational learning: a theory of action perspective,* Addison Wesley, Reading, Mass., 1978.

Ashton, D., Braiden, E., and Easterby-Smith, M., *Auditing management development,* Gower, Aldershot, 1980.

Barnard, C., *The functions of the executive,* Harvard University Press, Cambridge, Mass., 1938.

Beer, S., *Brain of the firm,* Herder and Herder, New York, 1972.

Bennis, W.G., and Nanus, B., *Leaders: the strategies for taking charge,* Harper and Row, New York, 1972.

Berne, E., *Games people play: the psychology of human relationships,* Grove Press, New York, 1964.

Berne, E., *The structure and dynamics of organizations,* Grove Press, New York, 1976.

Beveridge, W.E., *The interview in staff appraisal,* Allen and Unwin, London, 1975.

Blake, R., and Mouton, J.S., *The managerial grid*, Gulf Publishing, Houston, 1964.

Blau, P.M., and Scott, W.R., *Formal organizations*, Chandler, San Francisco, 1962.

Boyatzis, R., *The competent manager*, John Wiley, 1982.

Bradford, L.P., *Making meetings work*, University Associates, La Jolla, Ca., 1976.

Bradford, L.P., (ed.), *Group development*, University Associates, San Diego, 1978.

Buchholz, S., *Creating the high performance team*, Wiley, New York, 1987.

Burns, J. MacGregor, *Leadership*, Chaps 3 and 4, Harper and Row, New York, 1978.

Chandler, A., *Strategy and structure*, MIT Press, Cambridge, Mass., 1962.

Chandler, A., *The visible hand*, Harvard University Press, Cambridge, Mass., 1977.

Christopher, M., *Strategy search: a guide to marketing for chief executives and directors*, Gower, Aldershot, 1987.

Clarron, C.G., Eves S.M., and Fenner, E.C., *Behaviour: a guide for managers*, Macmillan, London, 1976.

Cleland, D., *Engineering team management*, Van Nostrand Reinhold, 1986.

Cohen, A.M., and Smith, R.D., *The critical incident in growth groups*, University Associates, San Diego, 1976.

Crosby, R.P., *Planning recommendations or actions: a team development guidebook*, University Associates, La Jolla, Ca., 1972.

Cyert, R.M., and March, J.G., *A behavioural theory of the firm*, Prentice-Hall, Englewood Cliffs, N.J., 1963.

Dalziel, M., *Changing ways*, American Management Association, New York, 1988.

Davis, S.M., and Lawrence, P.R., *Matrix*, Addison-Wesley, Reading, Mass., 1977.

Deal, T.E., and Kenedy, A.A., *Corporate cultures*, Addison-Wesley, Reading, Mass., 1982.

Dingwall, R., *Tools for team development*, EMAS Publishing, Crawley, 1980.

Drucker, P.F., *Managing for results*, Harper and Row, New York, 1964.

Dyar, D.A., and Giles, W.J., *Improving skills in working with people: interaction analysis,* HMSO, London, 1974.

Dyer, W.F., *Teambuilding issues and alternatives,* Addison-Wesley, Massachusetts and London, 1977.

Eddy, W.B., et al., *Behavioural science and the manager's role,* University Associates, La Jolla, Ca., 1976.

Ends, E.J., and Page, C.W., *Organisational teambuilding,* Winthrop, Cambridge, Mass., 1977.

Food Drink and Tobacco Industry Training Board, *Development at work,* Gloucester, 1978.

Forbes Greene, S., *The encyclopaedia of icebreakers,* Applied Skills Press, San Diego, 1983.

Fordyce, J.K., and Weil, R., *Managing with people,* Addison-Wesley, London, 1971.

Francis, D., and Woodcock, M., *50 Activities for self-development,* Gower, Aldershot, 1982.

Galbraith, J.R., *Designing complex organizations,* Addison-Wesley, Reading, Mass., 1973.

Guest, R., *Work teams and team building,* Pergamon Press, New York, 1986.

Hall, R.H., *Organizations: structure and process,* Prentice-Hall, Englewood Cliffs, N.J., 1982.

Hampden-Turner, C., *Maps of the mind,* Macmillan, New York, 1981.

Handy, C., *Gods of management,* Pan Books, London, 1978.

Honey, P., *Face to face: a practical guide to interactive skills,* 2nd ed., Gower, Aldershot, 1988.

James, M., and Jongeward, D., *Born to win,* Addison-Wesley, London, 1973.

Janis, I.L., *Victims of groupthink,* Houghton Mifflin, Boston, 1972.

Jay, M., *The dialectical imagination,* Heinemann, London, 1973.

Jones, J.E., and Pfeiffer, J.W., *Handbooks of structured experiences for human relations training,* University Associates, San Diego, Vols. 1 to 10, 1974–1985.

Jones, J.E., and Pfeiffer, J.W., *Instrumentation in human relations training,* University Associates, San Diego, 1976.

Jones, J.E., and Woodcock, M., *Manual of management development,* Gower, Aldershot, 1985.

Kanter, R.M., *The change masters,* Simon and Schuster, New York, 1983.

Kepner, C.H., and Treggoe, B.B., *The new rational manager,* John Martin Publishing, London, 1981.

Kilcourse, T., *Management team development: a problem-centred technique,* MCB Publications, 1984.

Kohler, W., *Gestalt psychology,* Liveright, New York, 1947, (originally published 1929).

Kotter, J.P., *The general managers,* The Free Press (divn of Macmillan Publishing), New York, 1982.

Lawrence, P.R., and Lorsch, J.W., *Developing organisations: diagnosis and action,* Addison-Wesley, Reading, Mass., 1969.

Lawrence, P.R., and Lorsch, J.W., *Organization and environment,* Harvard Graduate School of Business Administration, Cambridge, Mass., 1967.

Levinson, H., *Organizational diagnosis,* Harvard University Press, Cambridge, Mass., 1972.

Lewis, R., Paine, N., and Stevenson, A., *Team working – a guide to management development groups,* National Extension College, Cambridge, 1985.

Lievegoed, B.C.J., *The developing organization,* Tavistock, London, 1973.

Lippitt, G.L., *Visualising change,* University Associates, La Jolla, Ca., 1976.

Lippitt, G.L., This, L.E., and Bidwell, R.G., *Optimising human resources: readings in individual and organisational development,* Addison Wesley, London, 1971.

Lloyd, P.C., *Creating a management team to achieve specific results,* Industrial and Commercial Techniques, London, 1974.

McClelland, D., *Power: the inner-experience,* John Wiley, New York, 1975.

McCormack, M.H., *What they don't teach you at Harvard Business School,* Collins, Glasgow, 1984.

McGregor, D., *The human side of enterprise,* McGraw-Hill, Maidenhead, 1960.

Maccoby, M., *The gamesman,* Simon and Schuster, New York, 1976.

Maier, N.F., The appraisal interview: three basic approaches, University Associates, La Jolla, Ca., 1976.

Margerison, C.J., *Managing effective work groups,* McGraw-Hill, Maidenhead, 1973.

Maslow, A.H., *Toward a psychology of being,* Van Nostrand, New York, 1968.

Mason, R.O., and Mitroff, I., *Challenging strategic planning assumptions*, John Wiley, New York, 1981.

Mausner, H.F.B., and Snyderman, B., *The motivation to work*, John Wiley, New York, 1959.

Merry, U., and Allerhand, M., *Developing teams and organisations*, Addison-Wesley, London, 1977.

Miller, D., and Friesen, P.H., *Organisations: a quantum view*, Prentice-Hall, Englewood Cliffs, N.J., 1984.

Mintzberg, H., *The nature of managerial work*, Harper and Row, New York, 1973a.

Mintzberg, H., *The structuring of organizations*, Prentice-Hall, Englewood Cliffs, N.J., 1979.

Mintzberg, H., *Power in and around organizations*, Prentice-Hall, Englewood Cliffs, N.J., 1983.

Mintzberg, H., *Structure in fives*, Prentice-Hall, Englewood Cliffs, N.J., 1983.

Morgan, G., *Images of organization*, Sage Publications Inc., Beverley Hills, 1986.

Naisbitt, J., *Megatrends*, Warner, New York, 1982.

Ohmae, K., *The mind of the strategist*, Penguin Books, Harmondsworth, 1983.

Onchen, W., *Managing management time*, Prentice-Hall, London, 1984.

Ouchi, W., *Theory Z: how American business can meet the Japanese challenge*, Addison-Wesley, Reading, Mass., 1981.

Ouchi, W., *Theory Z*, Addison-Wesley, Reading, Mass., 1982.

Pascale, R.T., and Athos, A.G., *The art of Japanese management* Simon and Schuster, New York, 1981.

Peters, T.J., and Waterman, R.H. Jr., *In search of excellence*, Harper and Row, New York, 1982.

Pfeiffer, J.W., and Jones, J.E. *Annual handbooks for group facilitators*, 1972–89, University Associates, La Jolla, Ca.

Polster, E., and Polster, E., *Gestalt therapy integrated*, Brunner/Mazel, New York, 1973.

Porter, M.E., *Competitive advantage: creating and sustaining superior performance*, Free Press, New York, 1985.

Quinn, J.B., *Strategies for change*, Irwin, Homewood, Ill., 1980.

Rackham, N., and Morgan, T., *Behaviour analysis in training*, McGraw-Hill, Maidenhead, 1977.

Reddin, W.J., *Effective management by objectives*, Management Publications Ltd, London, 1971.

Rimler, G., *Small business: developing the winning management team*, American Management Association, Washington, 1980.

Roberts, T., *Developing effective managers*, Institute of Personnel Management, London, 1974.

Schein, E., *Organizational culture and leadership*, Jossey-Bass, San Francisco, 1985.

Schein, E., *Process consultation*, Addison-Wesley, Reading, Mass., 1969.

Schein, E., *Process consultation: its role in organizational development*, Addison-Wesley, Reading, Mass., 1969.

Schindler-Rainman, E., Lippitt, R., and Cole, J., *Taking your meetings out of the doldrums*, University Associates, La Jolla, Ca., 1977.

Smith, G.D., Arnold, D.R., and Bizzell, B.G., *Strategy and business policy*, Houghton Mifflin, Boston, 1985.

Snyder, R., *Organisational culture: the planning of change*, 4th ed., Holt, New York, 1985.

Spartz, D., *Management vitality: the team approach*, Society of Manufacturing Engineers, Publications/Marketing Services Division, Dearborn, Mich., 1984.

Sperry, L., and Hess, L.R., *Contact counselling: communication skills for people in organisations*, Addison-Wesley, London, 1974.

Srivastva, S., *The executive mind*, Jossey-Bass, London, 1983.

Toffler, A., *The third wave*, Bantam, New York, 1980.

Townsend, R., *Up the organisation*, Fawcett, New York, 1970.

Tregoe, B., and Zimmerman, J., *Top management strategy*, John Martin, London, 1980.

Urwick Orr and Partners and Clothing and Allied Products Training Board, *Improving management performance – summary of five case studies*, London, 1978.

Vanek, J., *Self mangement*, Penguin, Harmondsworth, 1975.

Vickers, G., *Value systems and social process*, Tavistock, London, 1965.

Vickers, G., *Human systems are different*, Harper and Row, New York, 1983.

Woodcock, M., *Team development manual*, 2nd ed., Gower, Aldershot, 1988.

Woodcock, M., and Francis, D., *Organisational development through teambuilding*, Gower, Aldershot, 1981.

Woodcock, M., and Francis, D., *The unblocked manager*, Gower, Aldershot, 1982.
Wynn, R., *Team Management: leadership by consensus*, Merrill, 1984.

Training journals

Australia

Training and Development in Australia, Australian Institute of Training and Development, PO Box 1011, Lalor, Victoria 3075.

Canada

Canadian Vocational Journal, Canadian Vocational Association, PO Box 3435, Station "D" Ottowa, Ontario KLP 614.

European

CEDEFOP News, European Centre for the Development of Vocational Training, Bundesallee 22 D-1000, Berlin 15.

France

Enterprises Formation, Association Nationale pour la Formation Professionnelle des Adults, 13 Place de Villiers, 93108 Montreuil.
Journal de la Formation Continue, 2 Rue d'Amsterdam, 75009 Paris.

Germany, West

Bulletin AIOSP, International Association for Educational and Vocational Guidance, c/o Friedrichstrasse, D-1000 Berlin 61.

Hong Kong

Vocational Training News, Vocational Training Council, 15 Floor, Harbour Centre, 25 Harbour Road, Wanchai.

India

Indian Journal of Training and Development, Indian Society for Training and Development, B41 Institutional Area South of IIT, New Delhi 110016.

Italy

Formazione e Lavoro, Ente Nazionale ACLI Istruzione Professionale, Via Giuseppe Marcora, 18 20 00153-Rome.

Japan

Industrial Training, Japan Industrial and Vocational Training Association, Nihon Sangyo Kunren Kyokai, 6th Floor, Minamizuka Building, 2-17-3 Shibuya, Tokyo 150.

South Africa

Journal for Technical and Vocational Education in South Africa, South African Association for Technical and Vocational Education, c/o Technician, Witwatersrand, PO Box 3293, Johannesburg 200.

UK

CBI Education and Training Bulletin, Confederation of British Industry, 102 New Oxford Street, London WC1A 1DU.

Journal of European Industrial Training, MCB University Press Ltd, 62 Toller Lane, Bradford, West Yorkshire BD8 9BY.

Training and Development, Institute of Training and Development Journals Ltd, 18 Pembroke Road, Kensington, London W8 6NT.

Training Digest, John Chittock, 37 Gower Street, London WC1E 6HH.

Training Officer, Marylebone Press Ltd, Lloyd's House, 18 Lloyd's St, Manchester M2 5WA.

Transition, Personnel Publications Ltd, 16 Park Crescent, London W1N 4AT.

US

Bulletin on Training, The Bureau of National Affairs Inc, 1231 25th Street NW, Washington DC 20037.

Employment and Training Reporter, The Bureau of National Affairs Inc. 1231 25th Street NW, Washington DC 20037.

Federal Trainer, US Office of Personnel Management, Training Resources Management Division-W E D 7230, Washington DC 20044.

Journal of Vocational Education Research, American Vocational Education Research Association, c/o Wesley E Budke, National Centre for Research in Vocational Education, Ohio State University, 1960 Kenny Road, Columbus, OH 43210.

Practical Supervision, Professional Training Associates Inc, 212 Commerce Boulevard, Round Rock, TX 78664.

Professional Trainer, McGraw-Hill Training Systems, Box 641, Del Mar, CA. 92014.

Training, Lakewood Publications Inc., 50 S 9th Street, Minneapolis, MN 55402.

Training and Development Alert, Advanced Personnel Systems, Box 1438, Roseville, CA 95661.

Training and Development Journal, American Society for Training and Development, 1630 Duke Street, No 13332, Alexandria, VA 22314.

Training News, Weingarten Publications Inc., 38 Chauncey Street, Boston, MA 02111.

Training Today, American Society for Training and Development, Chicagoland Chapter, 203 N Wabash Avenue, Ste 2210, Chicago, IL 60601.

Training Trends, TPC Training Systems, 1301 S Grove Avenue, Barrington, IL 60010.

Vocational Training, Capitol Publications Inc., 1300 N 17th Street, Arlington, VA 22209.

Management journals

UK

British Journal of Administrative Management, Institute of Administrative Management, 40 Chatsworth Parade, Petts Wood, Orpington BR5 1RW.

Business Matters, Whitehall Press Ltd, Earl House, Maidstone, Kent, ME14 1PE.

Chief Executive, Morgan-Grampian (Professional Press) Ltd, Calderwood Street, London SW18.

Director, Institute of Directors, Director of Publications Ltd, 116 Pall Mall, London SW1Y 5ED.

European Management Journal, Basil Blackwell Ltd, 108 Cowley Road, Oxford OX4 1JF.

Graduate Management Research, Cranfield School of Management, Cranfield Institute, Cranfield Press, Cranfield, Bedford MK43 0AL.

Journal of Managerial Psychology, MCB University Press Ltd, 62 Toller Lane, Bradford, West Yorkshire BD4 9BY.

Leadership and Organisational Development Journal, MCB University Press Ltd, 62 Toller Lane, Bradford, West Yorkshire BD4 9BY.

Management Education and Development, Association of Teachers of Management, Centre for the Study of Management Learning, University of Lancaster, Lancaster LA1 4YX.

Management in Government, HMSO, Atlantic House, Holborn Viaduct, London, EC1P 1BN.

Management Today, Management Publications Ltd, 30 Lancaster Gate, London W2 3LP.

Strategic Management Journal, John Wiley & Sons Ltd, Baffins Lane, Chichester, Sussex PO19 1UD.

US

Acadamy of Management Journal 1958, C30 Walter B. Newsome, Box KZ, Mississippi State, MS 39762.

Advanced Management Journal 1935, Society for Advancement of Management, 2331 Victoria Parkway, Cincinatti, OH 45206.

Association Management, American Society of Association Executives, 1575 Eyre Street, N.W., Washington D.C.

California Management Review, University of California, Berkeley School of Business Administration, 350 Barrows Hall, Berkeley, CA 94720.

Competitive Edge (Miramar), National Home Furnishings Association, 405 Merchandise Mart Plaza, Chicago, Il 60654.

Creative Management, Business Research Publications Inc., 817 Broadway, New York, NY 10003.

Fortune Magazine, Time Inc., Time & Life Building, 1271 Avenue of the Americas, New York, NY 10020.

Human Resource Management, John Wiley & Sons Inc., 605 Third Avenue, New York, NY 10158.

Industrial Management, Institute of Industrial Engineers, Industrial and Management Press, 25 Technology Park/Atlanta, Norcross, GA 30092.

Interaction (New York), Organizational Behaviour Institute (Subsidiary of B.F.S. Psychological Associates Inc.), 666 Fifth Avenue, New York, NY 10103.

Journal of Business Strategy, Warren, Goreham and Lamont Inc., 210 South Street, Boston, MA 02111.

Long Range Planning, Society for Long Range Planning, Pergamon Press Inc., Journals Division, Maxwells House, Fairview Park, Elmsford, New York, NY 10523.

McKinsey Quarterly, McKinsey & Co. Inc., 55 E. 52nd Street, New York, NY 10022.

Management Development Guide, American Management Association, 135 W. 50th Street, New York, NY 10020.

New Management, Wilson Learning Corporation, c/o Diane Ewart, 6950 Washington Avenue S., Eden Prairie, MN 55344.

Organizational Behaviour Teaching Review, Organizational Behaviour Teaching Society, University of Oklahoma, College of Business, Norman, OK 73019.

Organizational Dynamics, American Management Association, AMACOM Division, 135 W. 50 Street, New York 10020.

Sloan Management Review, Sloan Management Review Association, Massachusetts Institute of Technology, Alfred P. Sloan School of Management, 50 Memorial Drive, Cambridge, MA 02139.

Training, Lakewood Publications Inc., 50 S. 9th Street, Minneapolis, MN 55402.

Publishers

Publishers of books

UK

The following are publishers of management books. Lists of titles can be obtained from each.

W.H. Allen & Co. plc
44 Hill Street
London
W1X 8LB

Basil Blackwell Publisher Ltd
108 Cowley Road
Oxford OX4 1JF

Century Hutchinson
  Publishing Group
Brookmount House
62-65 Chandos Place
London
WC2N 4NW

Collins Publishers
8 Grafton Street
London
W1X 3LA

Gower Publishing Company
  Ltd
Gower House
Croft Road
Aldershot
GU11 3HR

William Heinemann Ltd
Halley Court
Jordan Hill
Oxford
OX2 8EJ

Institute of Personnel
  Management
IPM House
Camp Road
Wimbledon
London
SW19 4UW

Kogan Page Ltd
120 Pentonville Road
London
N1 9JN

Longman Group Ltd
Longman House
Burnt Mill
Harlow
Essex
CM20 2JE

McGraw-Hill Book Co.
  (UK) Ltd
McGraw-Hill House
Shoppenhangers Road
Maidenhead
Berks
SL6 2QL

MCB University Press Ltd
62 Toller Lane
Bradford
West Yorks
BD8 9BY

University Associates
  International Ltd
Challenge House
45-47 Victoria Street
Mansfield
Notts
NG18 5SU

John Wiley & Sons Ltd
Baffins Lane
Chichester
West Sussex
PO19 1UD

US

ACA Books
1285 Avenue of Americas
3rd floor Area M
New York
NY 10019

AMACOM Book Division
135 West 50th Street
New York
NY 10020-1201

American Arbitration
Association
140 W 51 Street
New York
NY 10020-1203

American Hospital Publishing
  Inc.
211 E Chicago Avenue
Chicago
IL 60611

American Sciences Press Inc.
20 Cross Road
Syracuse
NY 13224-2144

Asher-Gallant Press
201 Montrose Road
Westbury
NY 11590

Aspen Publishers Inc.
1600 Research Blvd
Rockville
MD 20850

Association of University
  Programs in Health
  Administration (AUPHA)
1191 N Fort Meyer Drive
Suite 503
Arlington
VA 22209

Atcom Inc. Publishers
2315 Broadway
New York
NY 10024

Auerback Publishers Inc.
One Penn Plaza
New York
NY 10119

Battelle Press
505 King Avenue
Colombus
OH 43201-2693

Bell Publishing
15 Surrey Lane East Brunswick
NJ 08816

BNA Books
1231 St NW
Washington
DC 2037

Bonus Books Inc.
160 E Illinois Street
Chicago
IL 60611

Branden Press Inc.
Box 843
17 Station Street
Brookline Village
Boston
MA 02147

Bridge Publications Inc.
1414 N Catalina Street
Los Angeles
CA 90027

Business & Legal Reports
64 Wall Street
Madison
CT 06443

Business Books Marketing
  Group
Box 6870-51 Torrance
CA 90504

Chatham House Publishers
  Inc.
Box One
Chatham
NJ 07928

Chilton Book Co.
Chilton Way
Radnor
PA 19089

The Conference Board Inc.
845 Third Avenue
New York
NY 10022

Consultants News
Templeton Road
Fitzwilliam
NH 03447

The Corinthian Press
3592 Lee Road
Shaker Heights
OH 44120

Crain Books NTC Business
  Books
4255 W Touhy Avenue
Lincolnwood
IL 60646

Crisp Publications Inc.
95 First Street
Los Altos
CA 94022

Dame Publications Inc.
7800 Bissonnet
Suite 415 Houston
TX 77074

The Dartnell Corp.
4660 Ravenswood Avenue
Chicago
IL 60640

Dorset House Publishing
   Co. Inc.
353 W 12 Street
New York
NY 10014

Executive Enterprises
   Publications Co. Inc.
22 W 21 Street
New York
NY 10010-6904

Fairchild Books & Visuals
7 E 12 Street
New York
NY 10003

The Fairmont Press Inc.
700 Indian Trial
Lilburn
GA 30247

Folio Publishing Corp.
Box 4949
6 River Bend
Stamford
CT 06840

Gulf Publishing Co.
Book Division
Box 2608
Houston
TX 77252

Harvard Business School Press
Morgan 41
Boston
MA 02163

Health Administration Press
1021 E Huron Street
Ann Arbor
MI 48104

Hive Publishing Co.
Box 1004
Alpha Building
Easton
PA 18042

Human Resource Development
   Press
22 Amherst Rd
Amherst
MA 01002

The ICC Publishing Corp. Inc.
156 Fifth Avenue
Suite 820
New York
NY 10010

IEE Press
345 E 47 Street
New York
NY 10017

ILR Press
Cornell University
Div of New York State School
   of Industrial & Labour
   Relations
Ithaca
NY 14851-0952

JAI Press Inc.
Box 1678
55 Old Post Road
Suite 2
Greenwich
CT 06836

Jossey-Bass Inc. Publishers
433 California Street
San Francisco
CA 94104

B. Klein Publications
Box 8503
Coral Springs
FL 33065

Kumarian Press Inc.
630 Oakwood Avenue
Suite 119
West Hartford
CT 06110

David S. Lake Publishers
19 Davis Drive
Belmont
CA 94002

Learning Resources Network
   (LERN)
Box 1448
Manhattan
KS 66502

Lomond Publications Inc.
Box 88
Mount Airy
MD 21771

Longman Financial Services
   Institute
520 N Dearborn
Chicago
IL 60610

McCutchan Publishing Corp.
2940 San Pablo Avenue
Berkeley
CA 94702

Management Resources Inc.
96 Morton Street
New York
NY 10014

Master Media Ltd
301 W 52 Street
3rd Floor
New York
NY 10019

Medical Economic Books
680 Kinderkamack Rd
Oradell
NJ 07649

Nichols Publishing Co.
PO Box 96
New York
NY 10024

Oliver Wright Ltd Publications
   Inc.
5 Oliver Wright Drive
Essex Junction
VT 05452

Omni Learning Institute
860 Merrimon Avenue
Suite 320
Asheville
NC 28804

Petrocelli Books Inc.
251 Wall Street
Research Park
Princeton
NJ 08540

Practice Management
  Associates Ltd
10 Midland Avenue
Newton
MA 02158

Probus Publishing Co.
118 N Clinton Street
Chicago
IL 60606

Productivity Press Inc.
Box 814
Cambridge
MA 02238

Ronin Publishing Inc.
Box 1035
Berkeley
CA 94701

Roxbury Publishing Co.
Box 491044
Los Angeles
CA 90049

Sage Publications Inc.
2111 W Hillcrest Drive
Newbury Park
CA 91320

Special Libraries Association
  (SLA)
1700 18 St N W
Washington
DC 20009

Syntony Publishing
1450 Byron Street
Palo Alta
CA 94301

The Taft Group
5130 MacArthur Blvd NW
Washington
DC 20016

Theatre Communications
  Group
355 Lexington Avenue
New York
NY 10017

Thompson & Co. Inc.
4600 Longfellow Avenue
Minneapolis
MN 55407-3638

University Associates Inc.
8517 Production Avenue
San Diego
California 92121

The Urban Institute Press
2100 'M' St NW
Washington
DC 20037

Van Nostrand Reinhold
  Co. Inc.
115 Fifth Avenue
New York
NY 10003

Whatever Publishing Inc.
58 Paul Drive
San Rafael
CA 94903

Markus Wiener Publishing Inc.
2901 Broadway
Suite 107
New York
NY 10025

Williamson Publishing Co.
Church Hill Road
Charlotte
VT 05445

Suppliers of management films and videos in the UK

BBC Enterprises Ltd
Woodlands
Wood Lane
W12 0TT
Tel: 01-743 5588
ext. 2232

CFL Vision.
Chalfont Grove
Gerrards Cross
Bucks
SL9 8TN
Tel: 02407 4433

Gower Training Resources
Gower House
Croft Road
Aldershot
GU11 3HR
Tel: 0252 331551

Guild Sound and Vision
6 Royce Road
Peterborough
PE1 5YB
Tel: 0733 315315

Industrial Society
Peter Runge House
3 Carlton House Terrace
London
SW1Y 5DG
Tel: 01-839 4300

Melrose Film Productions
8-12 Old Queen Street
London
SW1 9HP
Tel: 01-222 1744

Millbank Films Ltd
1 Adam Street
London
WC2N 6AW
Tel: 01-839 7176

Rank Training
PO Box 70
Great West Road
Brentford
Middlesex
TW8 9HR
Tel: 01-568 9222

University Associates
   International Limited
45-47 Victoria Street
Mansfield
Notts
NG18 5SU
Tel: 0623 640203

Video Arts
Dumbarton House
68 Oxford Street
London
W1N 9LA
Tel: 01-580 0652

Selected organizations – UK

Management training organizations

Aldwark Management Training
  Ltd
106 Micklegate
York
YO1 1JX
Tel: 0904 647728

Ashridge Management College
Berkhamsted
Hertfordshire
HP4 1NS
Tel: 044 284 3491

BACIE (British Association for
  Commercial and Industrial
  Education)
16 Park Crescent
London
W1N 4AP
Tel: 01-636 5351

BIS Applied Systems Ltd
20 Upper Ground
London
SE1 9PN
Tel: 01-633 0866

Barleythorpe Management
  Centre
Barleythorpe
Oakham
Leicestershire
LE15 7ED
Tel: 0572 3711

The Bradford Management
  Centre
Heaton Mount
Keighley Road
Bradford
West Yorkshire
BD9 4JU
Tel: 0274 42299

Brathay Hall Trust
Brathay Hall
Ambleside
Cumbria
LA22 0HP
Tel: 05394 33041

British Institute of
   Management
Management House
Cottingham Road
Corby
Northants
NN17 1TT
Tel: 0536 204222

Brunel University
Uxbridge
Middlesex
UB8 3PH
Tel: 0895 56461
ext 215

CMTC – Management
   Training Centre
Woodland Grange
Leamington Spa
CV32 6RN
Tel: 0926 36621/5

The City University Business
   School
Management Development
   Centre
Frobisher Crescent
Barbican Centre
London
EC2 8HB
Tel: 01-910 0111

The College of Management
Dunchurch
Rugby
Warwickshire
CV22 6QW
Tel: 0788 810656

Cranfield School of
   Management
Cranfield
Bedford
MK43 0AL
Tel: 0234 751122

Fielden House Productivity
   Centre Ltd
856 Wilmslow Road
Didsbury
Manchester
M20 8RY
Tel: 061-445 2426

Guardian Business Services
119 Farringdon Road
London
EC1R 3DA
Tel: 01-278 6787

Henley, The Management
   College
Greenlands
Henley-on-Thames
Oxon
RG9 3AU
Tel: 0491 571454

Hoskyns Group Ltd
Hoskyns House
130 Shaftesbury Avenue
London
W1V 7DN
Tel: 01-434 2171

Industrial Society
Peter Runge House
3 Carlton House Terrace
London
SW1Y 5DG
Tel: 01-839 4300

Institute of Directors
116 Pall Mall
London
SW1Y 5ED
Tel: 01-839 1233

Institute of Manpower Studies
University of Sussex
Mantell Building
Falmer
Brighton
BN1 9RF
Tel: 0273 686751

Institute of Personnel
  Management
IPM House
Camp Road
Wimbledon
London
SW19 4UW
Tel: 01-946 9100

The Leadership Trust
Weston-Under-Penyard
Ross-on-Wye
Herefordshire
HR9 7YH
Tel: 0989 67667

London Chamber of
  Commerce and Industry
69 Cannon Street
London
EC4N 5AB
Tel: 01-248 4444

London Graduate School of
  Business Studies
Sussex Place
Regent's Park
London
NW1 4SA
Tel: 01-262 5050

Manchester Business School
Booth Street West
Manchester
M15 6PB
Tel: 061-273 8228

The Open University
Walton Hall
Milton Keynes
MK7 6AA
Tel: 0908 74066

OTMA Ltd
Victoria House
Southampton Row
London
WC1B 4DH
Tel: 01-405 4730

Pera Training
Nottingham Road
Melton Mowbray
Leicestershire
LE13 0PB
Tel: 0664 501264

Reed International plc
Training and Development
  Department
College House
Aylesford
Maidstone
Kent
ME20 7PR
Tel: 0622 77777
ext. 4285

Richmond Consultants Limited
20 Ridgway
Mount Ararat Road
Richmond
Surrey
TW10 6PR
Tel: 01-948 0270

Roffey Park Management
  College
Forest Road
Horsham
West Sussex
RH12 4TD
Tel: 029383 644

St Helens School of
  Management Studies
Water Street
St Helens
Merseyside
WA10 1PZ
Tel: 0744 33766

Structured Training Limited
Concorde House
24 Warwick New Road
Royal Leamington Spa
CV32 5JH
Tel: 0926 37621/6

Sundridge Park Management
  Centre
Bromley
Kent
BR1 3TP
Tel: 01-460 8585

Tack Training International
Tack House
Longmore Street
London
SW1V 1JJ
Tel: 01-834 5001

Templeton College
The Oxford Centre for
  Management Studies
Kennington
Oxford
OX1 5NY
Tel: 0865 735422

Urwick Management Centre
Baylis House
Stoke Poges Lane
Slough
Berkshire
SL1 3PF
Tel: 0753 34111

West of England Management
  Centre
Engineers' House
The Promenade
Clifton Down
Bristol
BS8 3NB
Tel: 0272 731471

Management organizations

Association of Business
  Executives
3 Station Parade
Balham High Road
London
SW12 9AZ

Association of Business
  Managers and
  Administrators
23 Sunnybank Road
Manchester
M13 0XF

Association of Management
  Consulting Organizations
Confederation House
Kildare Street
Dublin 2

Association for Management
  Education and Development
Premier House
77 Oxford Street
London
W1R 1RB

British Institute of
  Management
Management House
Cottingham Road
Corby
Northamptonshire
NN17 1TT

Confederation of British
  Industry
Centre Point
103 New Oxford Street
London
WC1A 1DU

Foundation for Management
  Education
Sun Alliance House
New Inn Hall Street
Oxford
OX1 2QE

Industrial Society
Peter Runge House
3 Carlton House Terrace
London
SW1 5D9

Institute of Administrative
  Management
40 Chatsworth Parade
Petts Wood
Orpington
Kent
PR5 1RW

Institute of Directors
116 Pall Mall
London
SW17 5ED

Institute of Management
  Consultants
32-33 West Halkin Street
London
SW1X 8JL

Institute of Management
  Services
1 Cecil Court
London Road
Enfield
Middlesex
EN2 6DD

Institute of Management
  Specialists
14 Hamilton Terrace
Royal Leamington Spa
Warwickshire
CV32 4LZ

Institute of Manpower Studies
University of Sussex
Mantell Building
Falmer
Brighton
BN1 9RF

Institute of Personnel
  Management
IPM House
Camp Road
Wimbledon
London
SW19 4UW

Institution of Production
  Engineers
66 Little Ealing Lane
London
W5 4XX

Local Authorities Management
  Services and Computer
  Committee
3 Buckingham Gate
London
SW1E 6JH

Management Association of SE
  Scotland
3 Randolph Crescent
Edinburgh
EH3 7UD

Management Buy-out
  Association
c/o Melville Technologies Ltd
Spring Road
Letchworth
Herts

Management Consultants
  Association
11 West Halkin Street
London
SW1X 8JL

MBO Society
Underriver Farm
Underriver
Sevenoaks
Kent
TN15 0SJ

Society for Long Range
  Planning
15 Belgrave Square
London
SW1X 8PU

Industrial training boards

Industrial training boards are established under the provisions of
the Industrial Training Acts 1964 and 1982 for the purpose of
making provision for the training of persons over compulsory
school age for employment in industry and commerce. The
industrial training boards are constituted for Great Britain.
Northern Ireland has its own system of training boards,
established under the Industrial Training Act (Northern Ireland)
1964.

Under the Acts, the Secretary of State for Employment has
power to establish industrial training boards by making industrial
training orders, though he may not do so until he has consulted

representative associations of employers and employees in the field concerned. Such consultations are carried out on his behalf by the Manpower Services Commission.

Some have done valuable work in the area of teambuilding and can offer relevant publications, training events and advice but discretion should be exercised by the user. In particular, it is worth bearing in mind that:

1. Boards do not all have the same views about development needs in their industries.
2. Some boards have done little work in the team development area and do not have real expertise to offer.
3. The skill and experience of the adviser is all-important so do not be afraid to challenge and question his or her views and the advice given. An adviser will respect you for it, otherwise you are probably better off without the advice.

Some boards also offer an information service and will lend out useful publications.

The following is a complete list of industrial training boards:

Agricultural ITB
Bourne House
32-34 Beckenham Road
Beckenham
Kent
BR3 4PB
(Dir., D.C. Newman)

Clothing and Allied Products
  ITB
Tower House
Merrion Way
Leeds
LS2 8NY
(Chief exec., J.W. Dearden)

Construction ITB
Dewhurst House
24 West Smithfield
EC1A 9JA
(Sec., J.A. Reynolds, OBE)

Engineering ITB
PO Box 176
54 Clarendon Road
Watford
Herts
WD1 1LB
(Sec., E.P. Jones)

Hotel and Catering ITB
International House
High Street
Ealing
W5 5DB
(Sec., W.A. Heaney)

Local Government Training
  Board
Arndale House
Arndale Centre
Luton
Beds
LU1 2TS
(Dir., M.G. Clarke)

Man-Made Fibres Industry
   Training Advisory Board
Gable House
40 High Street
Rickmansworth
Herts
WD3 1ER
(Gen. manager, D.W. Ashby)

Plastic Processing
Coppice House
Halesfield 7
Telford
Shropshire
TF7 4NA
(Chief exec., J.C. Shearman)

Offshore Petroleum
Offshore Training Centre
Forties Road
Montrose
Angus
DD10 9ET
(Sec., P.J. Bing, OBE)

Management consultants

The two professional organizations for management consultancy
are:

The Management Consultants Association
11 West Halkin Street, London SW1W 8JL
Tel: 01-235 3897

The Institute of Management Consultants
32-33 Hatton Garden, London EC1N 8DL
Tel: 01-242 2140

The Management Consultancy Information Service maintains
files on management consultants in the UK and use of the
service is free. Address: 38 Blenheim Avenue, Gants Hill,
Ilford, Essex IG2 6JQ
Tel: 01-554 4695.

Business schools

Business schools offer postgraduate degree or equivalent courses
in management or business.

Ashridge Management College
Berkhamsted
Hertfordshire
HP4 1NS

University of Aston
Management Centre
Nelson Building
Gosta Green
Birmingham 54

University of Bath School of
    Management
Claverton Down
Bath
BA2 7AY

Queen's University of Belfast
Department of Business
    Studies
Belfast
Northern Ireland

University of Bradford
Management Centre
Emm Lane
Bradford
West Yorkshire
BD9 4JL

City University Business
    School
Frobisher Crescent
Barbican Centre
London
EC2Y 8HB

Cranfield Institute of
    Technology
Cranfield School of
    Management
Cranfield
Beds
MK43 0AL

Durham University Business
    School
Mill Lane
Durham
DH13 LB

University of Edinburgh
Scottish Business School
Department of Business
    Studies
William Robertson Building
50 George Square
Edinburgh
EH8 9JY

University of Glasgow
Division of the Scottish
    Business School
Glasgow

Henley, The Management
    College
Greenlands
Henley-on-Thames
Oxon
RG9 3AU

University of Hull
Department of Management
    Systems and Sciences
Hull
HU6X 7RX

The International Management
    Centre for Buckingham
Castle Street
Buckingham
Buckinghamshire
MK18 1BJ

University of Lancaster
Gillow House
Bailrigg
Lancaster
LA1 4YX

University of Leeds
Department of Management
  Studies
Leeds
LS2 9JT

London Graduate School of
  Business Studies
Sussex Place
Regent's Park
London NW1 4SA

London School of Economics
Houghton Street
London
WC2A 2AE

University of London
Imperial College
Management Science
  Department
London
SW7 2BX

Loughborough University of
  Technology
Department of Management
  Studies
Loughborough
Leicestershire
LE11 3TU

University of Manchester
Manchester Business School
Booth Street West
Manchester
M15 6PB

University of Manchester
Institute of Science and
  Technology
Department of Management
  Science
PO Box 88
Sackville St
Manchester
M60 1QD

University of Oxford
Templeton College
Oxford Centre for Management
  Studies
Kennington Road
Kennington
Oxford
OX1 5NY

University of Salford
Department of Business and
  Administration
Salford
M5 4WT

University of Sheffield
Division of Economic Studies
Sheffield
S10 2TN

University of Strathclyde
Business School
130 Rottenrow
Glasgow
G4 0GE

University of Wales Institute of
  Science and Technology
2 Museum Place
Cardiff
CF1 3BG

University of Warwick
School of Industrial and
  Business Studies
Coventry
Warwickshire
CV4 7AL

Other useful organizations

These are listed because they have publications, undertake assignments, give advice, run courses or supply information on human relations/teambuilding topics.

BACIE
16 Park Crescent
Regent's Park
London
W1N 4AP

British Institute of
  Management
Management House
Parker Street
London
WC2B 5PT

British Institute of
  Management
Cottingham Road
Corby
Northants
NN17 1TT

Confederation of British
  Industry
Centre Point
New Oxford Street
London
WC1A 1DU

Department of Employment
St James's Square
London
SW1Y 4JB

Group Relations Training
  Association
56 Millbank Road
Darlington
Co. Durham
DL3 9NH

Industrial Society
48 Bryanston Square
London
W1H 8AH
and
Peter Runge House
3 Carlton House Terrace
London
SW1Y 5DG

Institute of Personnel
  Management
IPM House
Camp Road
Wimbledon
London
SW19 4UW

National Economic
  Development Office
Millbank Tower
Millbank
London
SW1P 4QX

Organisation Development
  Network
ODN Secretariat
Hatchetts
Butchers Lane
Preston
Hitchin
Hertfordshire
SG4 7TR

The Training Agency
Moorfoot
Sheffield
S1 4PQ

Selected organizations – rest of world

Management organizations

Because of the wide differences in roles and the services offered it is difficult to categorize management organizations. However, for each of the principal countries of the world, the name and address of one or more organizations concerned with the development of management skills is given. These will, in most cases, be in a position to direct enquirers to other organizations where appropriate.

International

European Council of
    Management (CECIOS)
Secretary c/o RKW
Dusseldorfer Strasse 40
Postfach 58 67
6236 Eschborn 1

World Council of Management
    (CIOS)
c/o NIVE
Van Alkemadelaan 700
2597 AW The Hague
Netherlands

Algeria

Institut National de la
    Productivité et du
    Développement Industriel
    (INPED)
125 bis rue Didouche
Mourad
Algiers

Argentina

Institute Para el Desarrollo de
    Empresarios en Argentina
Moreno 1850
P piso
Buenos Aires

Australia

Australian Institute of
  Management
National Centre
Suite 18
65 Queens Road
Melbourne

Australian Management
  (Graduates) Society
GPO Box 230
Sydney
NSW 2001

Austria

United Nations Industrial
  Development Organisation
  (UNIDO)
PO Box 300
A-1400 Vienna

Bahamas

Bahamas Institute of
  Commerce
Heasties Building
Robinson Road
PO Box N7917
Nassau

Belgium

Association International
  d'Etudiants en Sciences
  Economiques et
  Commerciales (AIESC)
Ave. Adolphe Buyl 123
B-1050 Brussels

European Association of
  Management Training
  Centres
51 rue de la Concorde
Brussels 5

Management Centre Europe
4 Avenue des Arts
Brussels 4

European Institute for
  Advanced Studies
  in Management
Place Stephanie 20
B1050 Brussels

European Research Group on
  Management (ERGOM)
PrediKatrenberg 55
B3200 Kessel-10

Union Internationale
  Chretienne des Dirigeants
  D'Enterprise (UNIAPAC)
49 Avenue D'Auderghem
B-1040 Brussels

Botswana

Institute of Management
  Development
Botswana
PO Box 1357

Brazil

Instituto de Organizaçao
  Racional Do Trabalho
Praça Don Jose Gaspor 30
Sao Paulo

Canada

Canadian Institute of
  Management
2175 Sheppard Avenue East
Suite 110
Willowdale
Ontario
M2J 1W8

China

China Enterprise Management
  Association
Sanlihe
Fuxingmenwai
Beijing

Cyprus

Cyprus Productivity Centre
Ministry of Labour and Social
  Insurance
PO Box 536
Nicosia

Czechoslovakia

Czechoslovak Committee for
  Scientific Management
Director
Siroka 5
11001 Praha 1

Denmark

Danish Employers'
  Confederation
1503 Vestervoldgade 113
Copenhagen V

Egypt

Industrial Development Centre
  for Arab States
IDCAS
PO Box 1297
Cairo

Ethiopia

African Association for Public
  Administration and
  Management
PO Box 60087
Addis Ababa

Finland

Finnish Institute of
  Management
Director Kalevankatu 12
00100 Helsinki 10

France

Comité National De
  l'Organisation Française
3 Rue Cassette
Paris 6e

Association Française de
  Management (CNOF)
Director General
119 rue de Lille
75007 Paris

Centre International de
  Maintenance Industrielle
  (CIMI)
8 rue de l'Azin
41018 Blois Cedex

European Association for
Personnel Management
72 rue St Louis en l'lle
F-75004 Paris

European Federation of
Management Consultants
3 rue Leon Bonnat
F-75016 Paris

European Industrial Research
Management Association
(EIRMA)
38 Cours Albert 1 er
75 Paris 8

Institut Européen
d'Administration Des
Affaires (INSEAD)
Boulevard de Constance
77305 Fontainebleau
Cedex

Institut Européen pour la
Formation Professionnelle
28 Avenue Hoche
75008 Paris

Ghana

Ghana Institute of
Management and Public
Administration
Greenhill
PO Box 50
Achimota

Greece

Greek Management
Association
27v Sophias Avenue
Athens

Greek Productivity Centre
28 Kapodistriou St
10682 Athens

Guyana

Guyana Institute of
Management
c/o The Communications
Officer
Bauxite Industry Development
Corporation Ltd
71 Main and Murray Sts
PO Box 7
Georgetown

Hong Kong

Hong Kong Management
Association
Management House 3rd Floor
26 Canal Road West

Hungary

National Management
Development Centre
Konyves Kalman Korut 48-52
H-1476 Budapest VIII

India

All India Management
  Association
Management House Area
14 Institutional Area
Lodi Road
New Delhi 110 003

Indian Institute of
  Management
Diamond Harbour Road
PO Joka
via Calcutta

Institute of Business
  Management
MP Chapter Plot No 196
A Sector Indrapuri
Bhopal (MP)

Institute of Modern
  Management
30 Dr. Sundari Mohan Avenue
Calcutta 700014

National Productivity Council
Lodi Road
New Delhi 110 003

Indonesia

Akademi Keuangan Dan
Perbankan
Alanat
Dhalan Mugas No 1
Semarang

Ireland

Irish Management Institute
Director General
Sandyford Road
Dublin 14

Israel

Israel Institute of Productivity
Director
4 Henrietta Szold Street
Tel Aviv 61330

Israel Management Centre
PO Box 33033
Tel Aviv 61330

Italy

Ufficio Documentazione PRO
  (IFAP)
Piazza della Reppublica 59
Roma 00185

Fondazione Giovanni Agnelli
Via Ormea 37
1-10125 Torino

Jamaica

Jamaican Institute of
  Management
15 Hillcrest Avenue
Kingston

Japan

Foundation for Asian
  Management Development
1704 Mori Building No 17
1-26-5 Toranoman
Minato-Ku
Tokyo 105

International Management
  Association of Japan
Mori 10th Building
1-18-1 Toranoman
Minot Ku
Tokyo

Japan Management
Association
3-11-22 Shiba Park
Minato-Ku
Tokyo 105

Jordan

Arab Organisation of
Administration Sciences
PO Box 17159
Amman

Kenya

Kenya Institute of Management
College House
Koinange Street
PO Box 43706
Nairobi

Malaysia

Malaysian Institute of
Management
227 Jalan Ampang
Kuala Lumpur 16 03

Malaysian Association of
Productivity
133 A Jalan Gasing
Petaling Jaya
PO Box 557
Jalan Sultan

Mauritius

Mauritius Institute of
Management
Cerne House
13 La Chaussee
Port Louis

Mexico

Instituto Nacional De
Administracion Publica
(INAP)
Km 14.5 Carretera
Mexico-Toluca
Delegacion Cuajimalpa
CP 05110

Nepal

Institute of Management
Tribhuvan University
PO Box 1246
Kirtipur
Kathmandu

Netherlands

Netherlands Management
Association (NIVE)
Managing Director
Van Alkemadelaan 700
2597 AW Den Hagg

New Zealand

New Zealand Institute of
Management
Auckland Division
Management House
303 Manurau Road
Epsom
Auckland Box 26-001

Nigeria

International Institute of
Managerial Technology
PO Box 258
Owerri
Imo State

Nigerian Institute of
Management
22 Alhaji Murtala Animashaun
Close
Off Adelabu Street
Surulere
PO Box 2557
Lagos

Centre for Management
Development
Management Village
Shangisha
Off Lagos/Ibadan Expressway
Tollgate
PMB 21578 Ikeja
Lagos State

Norway

The Norwegian National
Committee of Scientific
Management
Wm. Thranesgt 98
Oslo 1

Pakistan

Pakistan Institute of
Management
Clifton
Karachi – 6

Papua New Guinea

Papua New Guinea Institute of
Management
PO Box 1010
Lae

Philippines

Asian Institute of Management
Eugenion Lopez Foundation
MCC PO Box 898
Makati
Rizal

Productivity and Development
Centre
DAP Building
San Miguel Avenue
Ortigas
Pasig
Metro Manila

Poland

Management Organisation and
Development Institute
UL Wawilska 56

Portugal

Centre De Formacao Tecnica
(LNETI)
Praca Principe Real 19
1200 Lisboa

Portuguese Management
Association (APM) President
Av. Casal Ribeiro 48-6 Dt
1000 Lisboa

Sierra Leone

Sierra Leone Institute of
Management
20 Lightfot Boston Street
PO Box 1426
Freetown

Singapore

Singapore Institute of
    Management
15 Scotts Road
04-02/13 Thong Teck Building
Singapore 0922

South Africa

The Manpower and
    Management Foundation of
    Southern Africa
Executive Director
PO Box 31993
Braamfontein

National Development and
    Management Foundation of
    South Africa
Management House
PO Box 31793
Braamfontein
Transvaal 2017

South African Institute of
    Management
PO Box 56222
Pinegowrie 2123
Transvaal

Institute of Personnel
    Management of South Africa
PO Box 31390
Braamfontein 2017

Soviet Union

Comecon Institute of
    Management
Prospekt Kalinina 56
Moscow 121205 USSR

Spain

Circulo De Empresarios
Serrano Jower 5-2
28015 Madrid

Sweden

The Swedish Institute of
    Management
Director General
PO Box 6501
11383 Stockholm

Switzerland

International Management
    Development Institute
4 Chemin De Conches
Geneva CH-1231

European Management Forum
19 Chemin des Hauts-Crets
Cobgny
Geneva CH-1223

International Management
    Institute Geneva
4 Chemin de Conches
Geneva CH-1231

Management Development
    Institute (IMEDE)
PO Box 1059/MSF
Lausanne CH-1001

Taiwan

China Productivity Centre
11th Floor
201-26 Tun Hua North Road
Taipei
Taiwan 105 ROC

Tanzania

Eastern and Southern African
  Management Institute Esami
PO Box 3030
Arusha

Thailand

Thailand Management
  Association
Samaggi Insurance Building
3rd Floor, Room No 5
308 Silom Road
Bangkok 10500

Trinidad

Management Development
  Centre Trinidad
PO Box 1301
Port of Spain

Tunisia

Industrial Center for Arab
  States
14 rue Yahia B Amor
Tunis

US

Administrative Management
  Society
Willow Grove
Pennsylvania
PA 19090

American Assembly of
  Collegiate Schools
  of Business
605 Ballas Road
Suite 220
St Louis
Missouri 63141

American Association of
  Industrial Management
2500 Office Centre
Maryland Road
Willow Grove
Pennsylvania
PA 19090

American Management
  Associations
135 West 50 Street
New York
NY 10020

American Society for Training
  and Development
1630 Duke Street
No 13332
Alexandria
VA 22314

Association of Systems
  Management
24587 Bagley Road
Cleveland
Ohio
OH 44138

Institute of Management
  Sciences
146 Westminster Street
Providence
Rhode Island
RI 02903

Institute of Public
  Administration
55 West 44th Street
New York
NY 10036

The Conference Board
845 Third Avenue
New York
NY 10022

The Council for International
  Progress in Management
  (US) Inc (CIPM)
845 Third Avenue
New York

West Germany

Association for Work Study
  and Industrial Organisation
  (REFA)
Wittichstrasse 2
Postfach 4138
6100 Darmstadt

International Institute of
  Management
Science Center Berlin
Platz de Luftbrucke
1-3 D-1000 Berlin 42

Zambia

Zambia Federation of
  Employers
Permanent House
Cairo Road
Lusaka

Zimbabwe

Zimbabwe Institute of
  Management
7th Floor
Inslip House
Samara Machel Avenue
Harare
PO Box 3733

Business schools

Business schools offer postgraduate degree or equivalent courses
in management or business.

Australia

University of Melbourne
Graduate School of Business
  Administration
Parkville
Victoria 3052

University of New South Wales
Australian School of
  Management
P.O. Box 1
Kensington
Sydney 2033

Belgium

Catholic University of Leuven
Department of Applied
   Economic Sciences
Dekenstraat 2
B-3000 Leuven

Université Catholique De
   Louvain
Institut d'Administration et de
   Gestion
Avenue de l'Espinette 16
B1348
Louvain-la-Neuve

Canada

McGill University
1001 Sherbrooke St. W.
Montreal
Quebec
H3A 1G5

McMaster University
Faculty of Business
Hamilton
Ontario
L8S 4M4

Queen's University at Kingston
School of Business
Kingston
Ontario
K7L 3N6

University of Western Ontario
School of Business
   Administration
Ontario
London
N6A 3K7

Faculty of Administrative
   Studies
York University
4700 Keele St
Toronto
Ontario
M3J IP3

France

Insead-European Institute of
   Business Administration
Boulevard de Constance
F-77305 Fontainebleau Cedex

South Africa

University of Cape Town
The Graduate School of
   Business
Private Bag
Rondebosch 7700
Cape Town

University of Witwatersrand
Graduate School of Business
   Administration
2 St Davids Place
Parktown
Johannesburg

Spain

Iese
University of Navarra
Avenida Pearson 21
Barcelona

Switzerland

Imede-Management
  Development Institute
23 Chemin de Bellerive
Lausanne CH-1007

IMI-International Management
  Institute
4 Chemin de Conches
Geneva CH-1231

US

University of California
  Berkeley
Graduate School of Business
  Administration
350 Barrows Hall
Berkeley
CA 94720

University of California
Los Angeles
UCLA Graduate School of
  Management
405 Hilgard Avenue
Los Angeles
CA 90024

Carnegie-Mellon University
Schenley Park
Pittsburgh
Pennsylvania

University of Chicago
Graduate School of Business
1101 E.58th Street
Chicago
Illinois 60637

Columbia University
Graduate School of Business
105 Uris Hall
New York
NY 10027

Cornell University
Graduate School of Business
  and Public Administration
Ithaca
NY 14853

Dartmouth College
Amos Tuck School of Business
  Administration
Hanover
New Hampshire
03755

Harvard University
Graduate School of Business
  Administration
Boston
Massachusetts

University of Illinois
Department of Business
  Administration
219 Commerce West
Urbana
Illinois 61801

Indiana University
Bloomington
Indiana 47405

University of Kansas
202 Summerfield Hall
Lawrence
Kansas

Massachusetts Institute of
Technology
Sloan School of Management
Cambridge
Massachusetts

University of Michigan
Graduate School of Business
Administration
Ann Arbor
Michigan

New York University
Graduate School of Business
Administration
100 Trinity Place
New York City
NY 10006

J.L. Kellogg Graduate School
of Management
Northwestern University
Leverone Hall
Evanston
Illinois 60201

Pace University
Graduate School of Business
Pace Plaza
New York
NY 10038

University of Pennsylvania
Wharton Graduate Division
The Wharton School
102 Vance Hall CS
PA 19104

University of Pittsburgh
Graduate School of Business
Pittsburgh
PA 15260

University of Southern
California
Graduate School of Business
University Park
Los Angeles
CA 90007

Stanford University
Graduate School of Business
Stanford
CA 94305

University of Virginia
The Colgate Darden
Graduate School of Business
Administration
Box 6550
Charlottesville
VA 22906